The Software Bug Book

Thoughts on Software Quality

Bill Marjerison

Copyright

Table of Contents

Tables and Figures

Introduction

In the process of software development, a certain number of flaws ("bugs") are certain to arise. These can lead to product delays and cost overruns, but can also lead to customer dissatisfaction or even physical harm if they happen to get out of the laboratory.

Developing software, project management, and selling software applications are entirely different skills sets. It is important that everyone understand each other for the team to achieve success, and this book is intended to provide some insight, largely from the developer's point of view.

For the developer, this book explains some of the causes of the more complex bugs, how to detect them, and how to fix them. I hope you will glean some additional insight into some of the heavier bugs, and also pick up some new development tips.

For managers and sales people, this book introduces some jargon that you should be familiar with, introduces "bugs" in an easy-to-understand way, and gives insight into what to realistically expect from developers.

For everyone, there are discussions of development methodologies. I hope these will give you some ideas on how to get everybody thinking on the same plane, and hopefully to minimize bugs in the process.

About Me

I am an American expatriate, living in Japan for more than thirty years. My college degree is in Business Administration, but I am a tinkerer at heart, and I spent most of my fun time in college in the Computer Science program. (That study included just enough Electrical Engineering to be dangerous.)

It turns out that programming is a fantastic way of making things, but unlike other "hobbies", you don't need any physical materials like transistors, chemicals, or paint. The materials are your ideas, which are free. Well, ok, in those days a computer cost a million dollars, but that was a transparent cost to me at the time.

I have been making my living in this industry for forty years now. I still program quite a lot, but not as furiously as I did when I was twenty or thirty years old.

I had the idea for the basic part of this book years ago, and originally it was just supposed to be about bugs. That turned out to be not enough material for an entire book, so I started adding additional, related topics, that I hope you will find of interest, and save you some research time.

Notes

- In this book I use the term "developer", "programmer", and "engineer" interchangeably.
- When I refer to GNU, I am generally referring to the GNU gcc and g++ compilers.

Chapter 1: Why do Bugs Happen?

Software development is neither an art nor a science, and unfortunately lacks the discipline used in other branches of engineering.

This chapter is an introduction to what you are trying to achieve before you release a software application.

Testing: Validation vs. Verification

Validation is the process of determining if you have created what you actually wanted.

The process usually involves the original developers, some internal "testers", and eventually end users. From a technical perspective, this means that the application program accepts the expected inputs and generates the expected outputs. And, from a user's perspective validation usually means that the application is easy to use and performs fairly well. The primary reason for validation failure is often rooted in a poor specifications or unrealistic development schedules.

Verification is the process of determining if the thing you built has been *implemented* correctly according to the specifications and the tools that were used. In the best case, an application can be both verified (it works), and validated (it turned out to be what you wanted). However, mistakes or misunderstanding during development can lead to a mismatch.

Verification can expose two kinds of problems:

- Simple bugs such as calculating the wrong value, forgetting to save some results in a file, and so on. These sometimes are handed back to the original developer, but oftentimes are simple mistakes that can be delegated to a junior person for correction.

- Program language-specific (e.g., C/C++) bugs. Not following the rules of the programming language perfectly results in erratic behavior, performance degradation, lost data, or total program failure. This category of bugs is the focus of this book.

Development Environment

Let's consider three development environments, and how the environment can lead to bugs.

Dream Development Environment

Assignment: Send a man to the moon.

Budget: Unlimited.

Time limit: Before the end of the decade would be nice.

Staffing: Hire as many geniuses as you want to.

Development Process:

- Brainstorm some potential rocket designs. Assign hundreds of specialists to each portion of the puzzle.

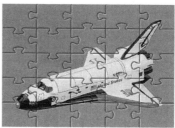

- Build prototypes, test, refine. A few prototypes may literally blow up, but that is anticipated in the budget.
- Decide final design, developing millions of pages of detailed specifications.
- Build it.
- Go to the moon.
- Done.

Strict Development Environment

Assignment: Make a smart box that goes into a car or an airplane.

Budget: Large, but not unlimited.

Time limit: One year. The box won't actually make it into a production model for a few years until regulatory hurdles have been cleared, but next year the same software people will be working on something else.

Staffing: Huge, especially for testing and for creating documentation required for ISO 26262, DO-178, or other set of rules.

Development Process:

- High-level system design, typically using tools such as a Unified Modeling Language system to generate the application template and documentation.

Designed by Committee?

- Mid-level sub-system design.
- Low-level module design and coding.
- Low-level module unit test.
- Mid-level sub-system unit test.
- High-level system test.
- Done; start project for next model year.

Typical Development Environment
Assignment: Make this thing where the screwball concept is written on a cocktail napkin.

Budget: Almost none.

Time limit: Before we go out of business or are destroyed by our competition, yesterday would be better.

Staffing: Never enough, but our team is very clever and very dedicated.

6

Development Process:

- Decipher the napkin; assign portions of the puzzle based on who's got experience in different areas (communications, database, user interface, etc.)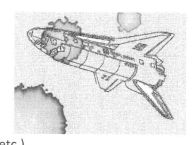
- Try to deal with the sales people who are selling it already, even though we don't know what it is yet.
- Build prototypes, test, refine. Observation: This is beginning to resemble a rocket.
- Boss changes the idea every other day and asks everybody to hurry up.
- It almost works! Let's go to the moon.
- Write final specification. Start sales.
- Begin version 4.0 (the marketing department asked you to skip versions 2 and 3 to give the image that this is a mature product).

In any of these scenarios, program defects are bound to occur. The severity of the defects depends on the skill of the developers, the work environment, time constraints, amount of testing done, and the tools that are employed.

The Goal

The goal in any development project is to make a perfect application that everybody loves, and will make you rich and famous. However, in the process, bugs happen. Why?

Creating software is somewhat like hyper-gourmet cooking. You may have a recipe that is a million lines long and has thousands of ingredients. You also have to deal with limited hardware. For example, my oven seems to have two settings: "off" and "inferno". Additionally, you sometimes have to deal with unexpected real time conditions such as when the rotating rack in my oven fails to turn properly, so things in the back get burnt to a crisp.

If you add *all* of the ingredients *at the right time* (and the oven rack does not get stuck), you can create a masterpiece that everybody gobbles up in one sitting. Miss one step and you have to eat the Carbon Blob Casserole all by yourself for an entire week.

Some trivia:
The collected works of William Shakespeare are about 118,800 lines long, and contain 3,392 decision points (i.e., the word "if" appears that many times). This does not include indirect decision points such as "To be or not to be…" and "Wherefore art thou Romeo?"

One of my applications that "only" makes phone calls is 253,820 lines of code, and has 10,285 "if" statements.

An Android-based device contains on the order of seven million lines of C/C++. Searching all of the C/C++-related files in the full code base reveals more than 768,000 "if" statements.

An automobile may easily have 100 or more processors with tens of millions of lines of code. Major components to control the engine, transmission, and so on each contain 200,000 to 1,000,000 lines of code.

A Cheese Soufflé must be easy: it's only five steps with eight ingredients.

Complicating software development can be:

- You are inventing a new technology (trying out a new or original recipe), so you are not sure what this is yet.
- Specifications are non-existent, vague, or just plain wrong.
- There are almost always multiple ways to solve the problem, which is to say that there are different recipes and different ways of cooking the same thing. The procedures you use are known as "algorithms". Some are well known, but your unique algorithms are what distinguish your product.
- Development in the old days mostly meant being able to express a solution for a particular specialty business, scientific, or engineering field as a computer program. These days there is much more involved such as creating the installation package, creating a help system, localization for world markets, creation of graphic elements for the user interface, and other areas that are not directly related to coding.
- The application has to do something useful in an efficient way—it is usually not enough that a few people like it.
- It is not yet clear exactly how people are going to use this, so the specifications may not meet end-user expectations.
- If you do a halfway decent job, people immediately want even more features, so the application can never be completed.

It is simply impossible, even for the best engineers, to keep all of the product requirements, computer tricks, and other details in their heads. So, with time constraints and all of the above, inappropriate or just plain incorrect program logic invariably creeps in. In the case of cooking this might mean forgetting to add a key ingredient or failing to mix something enough. For example, oops—I forgot to add the yeast to the bread!

Writing the actual code (mixing the ingredients) is rather easy, but making the entire casserole come out perfectly requires a lot of skill, luck, and a small dose of black magic. The parts that do not work together *as expected* are called "bugs". Some bugs you can live with—provided that they do not have serious consequences for the user.

Of course I am poking fun at the "Typical Development Environment"; I am unfortunately very familiar with it. You can have a lot of smart staff, but without proper tools, development methodology, and time, you are likely to start out with a lot of bugs.

I also feel bad for people who have to develop in the "Strict Development Environment". The huge amount of test code that you have to write will limit the number of bugs, but doing this is a totally uninteresting and thankless job, so it is probably difficult to keep the staff around for very long.

However, bugs can happen even in a "Dream" environment due to plain human error. Does anyone remember the Mars Climate Orbiter, where somebody mixed up English and metric units? Needless to say, $125 million dollars was literally lost in space.

In Chapter 4: Software Development Methodology, I'll talk more about development methodologies in a less facetious tone.

Chapter Summary

"Bugs" happen because "us software guys" are trying to do something very complicated, frequently under an obscene schedule and in an unfavorable environment.

Chapter 2: Instant Computer Science

This chapter is primarily for non-developers, and introduces some useful concepts and jargon. Topics include types of applications (desktop, cloud, embedded, mobile, etc.), programming languages, processors, processes, and threads.

Types of Applications

Below are some general categories of computer software applications.

Table 1 - Types of Applications

Type	Description
Desktop	Generally, an application that supports a business process functionality such as word processing, spreadsheet, accounting, reporting, and so on, and runs standalone on the user's desktop computer.
Web	Applications based on HTML, where the user submits a query over the Internet, a "Web Server" looks up the answer and responds with a formatted reply. Basic Web applications are only connected to the server during the request-reply phase. More advanced applications may establish additional, long-term connections to provide, for example, audio and video on demand.
Mobile	Applications that run on a tablet, smartphone, or other kind of portable computer. These often provide the same functionality as Desktop applications, but with a different user interface and typically

	a limited input capability.
Cloud	A hybrid model where Desktop applications and services such as file storage are run on a centralized server that is accessed using Web technology. Computers have essentially become too fast for ordinary users who only want to play with the Internet and do a little word processing. Cloud service companies can now offer complete *virtual machines* to users for use as web and e-commerce servers as well as for general computing—at a fraction of the cost of owning your own system.
Embedded	Applications hidden inside a device that doesn't look like a computer such as a microwave oven or the anti-skid braking system in a car.
Games	A very saturated market with hundreds of thousands of developers. Games range from free ("well, it was fun to do"), to $60 for console games for PlayStation and XBox, to thousands of dollars per user for business simulation games. It is nearly impossible to get any market exposure or to make any money unless you are lucky or have millions of dollars to spend on marketing.
Engineering and Scientific	Applications that typically use advanced mathematics to design or model complex physical entities and systems such as atomic reactions,

	weather, electronic circuits, buildings, airplanes, and so on.
Development Tools	Applications that help developers create other applications. This includes compilers, linkers, debuggers, editors, analysis tools, and others.
Operating Systems	The basic application that runs other applications.

Processors Galore

The Central Processing Unit (CPU, or just "processor") is the "engine" for the computer system. Forty years ago, a computer system required the same space as several buses. Compare this to your smartphone or tablet computer which is probably more powerful. There are also processors inside credit cards these days, and I always have trouble at the electronics parts shop finding the 5mm^2 microprocessor chips. (Just kidding—these are too small to work with. You actually buy these on rolls of tape so they can installed by robotic equipment.)

If you need low-cost microprocessors with low power consumption and lots of built-in sensors, I feel sorry for you. There are a zillion devices to choose from! Last time I looked, one manufacturer I know was offering more than 500 variations, so you can spend many hours just trying to find what you want. (Fortunately, most companies like this have a "wizard" tool to help you decide.) A lot of product research can save you a lot of money in both parts and design cost if you want to build a million toaster ovens.

If you are building something that requires more power than a toaster oven, you are most likely to run into in these types of processors.

Table 2 – Common Processors

Processor	Description
ARM	ARM Holdings is a U.K. company that only designs low-power, high-performance processors for embedded applications. ARM is a "fabless" company, that is, they do not have fabrication facilities. Instead, they license their designs to companies who actually have semiconductor factories. Worldwide, there are currently about twenty major companies producing ARM-based chip sets (the processor + some added value such as a telephone interface). Most everything in a smartphone or a tablet these days has an ARM-based design.
Atom	Atom is Intel's low-power version of the x86/x86-64 (see below), and is their attempt to wrest market share away from ARM. With few design wins in its five-year history, Intel is now pinning its hopes on the Atom's successor, the "Silvermont", which offers higher performance and lower power consumption.
M68K	In the 1980s and early 1990s, this Motorola "M68000" architecture pretty much led to the creation of the "low-cost engineering workstation" market. The Motorola semiconductor division was spun off as "Freescale", and you can still find this architecture rebranded as "ColdFire" and "DragonBall".
MIPS	This architecture was developed out of some research at Standard University. The company has a very complex history, and currently exists as a fabless design company. Their designs are currently used in some embedded applications, but the future of this architecture is unclear.
PowerPC (PPC)	This family of processors was developed jointly by Apple, IBM, and Motorola, to both create a better processor, and also, I presume, to stop letting Intel make so much money. Apple dropped out of this alliance in 2005 and switched to Intel architecture. This move certainly put a nail in the coffin of this architecture. Newer PPCs with "Cell Architecture" are used in Sony PlayStations, which is probably the only thing that keeps this architecture alive. From what I have read, it is a very difficult to program the "Cell" feature.
SPARC	A chip that originated at Sun Microsystems, now a division of Oracle. A number of companies manufacture SPARC-based processors.
SuperH	This family of chips from Renesas was originally developed by Hitachi. They are used in embedded applications,

	particularly in the automotive industry.
v850	This family of chips from Renesas was originally developed by NEC. They are used in embedded applications, including multi-media and automotive applications.
x86	This is the Intel architecture that started the PC revolution.
x86-64	This is the 64-bit version of the x86 architecture. While Intel was developing the Itanium series to replace the x86, AMD developed the x86-64 extensions. The Itanium never took off, and Intel, too, adopted the X86-64.

The processor used will be decided by:

- Capacity. 8-bit, 16-bit, 32-bit, and 64-bit processors can access different amounts of memory. More "bits" usually implies faster processing, too.
- Speed. The raw "clock speed" indicates how many instructions per second can be executed. Beware, however, that you cannot compare clock speeds from different architectures because the instruction sets are different.
- Number of cores. Newer high-end processors typically contain multiple cores to support multiple threads of execution directly in the hardware.
- Internal familiarity with the architecture.
- Application-specific features. Processors for embedded applications usually contain features for specific applications that make it easier to connect to external devices. For example, some processors are better than others for building a DVD player.
- Price.

It is not necessary to know the details of these or other processors, but it's useful to have a few of names in the back of your head when you are in a meeting.

Programming Languages

To get a computer to do anything useful, you have to write a program to instruct it what to do. Some choices for programming languages are shown below.

Table 3 - Partial List of Programming Languages

High-level	Adam, Algol, APL, BLISS, C, C++, C# (Sharp), COBOL, Eiffel, Forth, FORTRAN, Haskell, Java, JavaScript, Jovial, Lisp, ML, Modula, Oberon, OCaml, Pascal, Perl, PL/1, Prolog, Python, Ruby, Simulate, Smalltalk, SNOBOL, Visual Basic, and others.
Low-level	Assembler language.
Lowest level	Machine language.

Major terminology that you ought to be familiar with is in regards to programming languages is described below starting with lowest level.

Machine Language

This is the lowest level of programming where you have to input raw machine instructions from some toggle switches or from a "sophisticated" input device such as a paper tape reader. The "machine" part means a particular processor. The machine instructions are numbers that the machine interprets to perform some very simple actions. For example a 5 might mean "add", and a 12 might mean "clear" (set to zero).

With only these simple instructions, how do you make a fancy, multi-color document with graphics, tables, automatic table of contents, and so on? Basically, you don't do this anymore. These days, if a chip maker comes out with an entirely new architecture and instruction set, people create emulators and cross-compilers so they can write the initial code in something less torturous than machine language.

Assembler Language

Assembler Language is a step above Machine Language because meaningful names are assigned to the instructions (you enter "add", not 5), and enter the instruction sequence into a text file, which is slightly readable by a highly-trained human. Then you run a program called the *"assembler"*, which turns this *source code* (the original "symbolic instructions") into an intermediate *"object"* file.

Next, you combine all of your object files with a *"linker"* program to create the *executable* file (the application), which contains the bits and bytes that the machine actually understands. The only possible way to write assembler or machine code is to be intimately familiar with how the particular processor works.

The use of assembler language these days is very limited, and is often restricted to the few pieces of software that needs to talk directly to the hardware, and it is either impossible or inefficient to do so in a High-level programming language.

High-level Language

High-level languages are those that are closer to natural language, and allow you to express complex operations with a small amount of code. Capabilities vary by language, how modern that language is, and by what problem the language designers were trying to solve. In any case, High-level languages let you work with an *abstract* machine, rather than a specific piece of hardware. This allows the programmer to concentrate more on solving the problem at hand, and to spend less time fiddling with the machine.

18

Some High-level languages are interpreted. The human-readable source code is decoded and then converted to machine language on-the-fly.

Most High-level languages are *compiled*, though. The *compiler* converts the source code either directly to object code, or sometimes to Assembler Language and then the compiler runs the assembler for you. With either technique you eventually end up with the *executable* file. This avoids the overhead of interpreting the source code each time, so naturally the program runs faster. Computers are so fast these days that compiling versus interpreting does not make much difference for small applications, but it does make a difference for large programs that you use every day such as a word processor.

Finally, High-level languages usually come with a *"runtime"* library. This is the collection of code that glues together the High-level language statements with the underlying operating system to handle things like file input and output. When an application says "Print 'Hi, Mom.'", there are all kinds of contortions that go on under the hood to actually make this happen.

The C and C++ Languages
The "C" language invented in 1972, is one of the most popular programming languages of all time. The generated code is compact and efficient, but the programmer still can get very close the machine level if necessary. At the time it was invented, "C" was considered to be a rather High-level language, although that is somewhat laughable when "C" is compared to newer languages.

"C++" was initially developed in 1979, and started becoming popular in the mid to late 90's. C++ extended the "C" language by adding many features including *classes, templates, multiple inheritance, virtual functions,* and *exception handling,* for which the interested reader can find discussions of on the Internet.

C++ is frequently used when memory is not a constraint, while "C" is used when memory is tight such as in an embedded application. Also, if you don't need the extra features of C++, "C" has slight performance advantage.

No matter what language the program is written in, the instructions and the data are, of course, stored in memory, and each memory cell has an *address* numbered from 0 to the size of memory – 1. The major fundamental unit of data storage is a "byte", which is group of "bits" (binary digits, or simply on-off switches). A byte is 8-bits long on most processors, and usually corresponds to the space required to store a single character in the ASCII character set. (Modern systems support multiple, complex character sets, so a character can occupy 2, 3, or 4 bytes when "Unicode" or other character sets are involved.) Bytes can be combined into other groupings such as "words" that can store larger objects such as numbers.

In many languages, the programmer is never aware where things are stored. However, in "C" and other languages you can access something indirectly by storing its address in a *"pointer"* variable, and pretty much do anything you please to the object at that address. The benefit of pointers is that instead of copying "TheHumongousCustomerDataTable" so another procedure can use it, you can just pass a more compact pointer to that data. This reduces the overhead of setting up the procedure call from "humongous" to only a few bytes, and the called procedure then can refer indirectly to the real data via the pointer.

Procedures, Functions, and Subroutines
Realistic applications are divided up into manageable chunks of code: modules (a set of related features such as "math", "file handling", or "graphics"), files (the "graphics" module might be split into individual files for different kinds of graphs, different brands of graphic chips, etc.), and each file may contain one or more *procedures* (short pieces of code that perform specific, frequently used calculations).

A "procedure" is the generic term for either a *"function"* that returns a value (e.g., "SquareRoot"), or a *"subroutine"* that does performs some action, but does not have any inherent information to return (e.g., "SystemShutdown").

Processes and Threads
A "process" is an executing set of procedures (i.e., a running "program"). On a simple processor in a microwave oven, for example, there is probably one process that is both the operating system and the application.

In a more sophisticated system, the operating system is responsible for managing multiple processes, and for arbitrating the use of system resources between those processes. Such resources include memory, files, display, keyboard, mouse, fixed and removable disk drives, network devices, and many others. And, of course, the operating system is also responsible for scheduling access to the CPU(s). In other words, the operating system is the master caretaker of all of the programs being used.

On a modern processor with *memory protection*, each process runs in its own *protected* address space that is not accessible by other processes. This prevents one process from accidentally (or intentionally, as with a virus) interfering with another process. If processes need to communicate with each other, they typically do so using some kind of *inter-process communication* mechanism such as pipes, sockets, files, remote procedure call, or shared memory.

A "thread" is an entry point into a process. A simple process is usually *single-threaded*: It starts at the "main procedure", does it thing, and exits. An important distinction between threads and processes is that threads all run within the *same* address space. This allows threads to communicate with each other directly through memory with almost no overhead.

Other important distinctions are that there is less overhead in creating a new thread than for creating a new process, and that switching between threads is faster than switching between processes because less information needs to be saved.

My Incredible Application
• Main Thread
• Database Thread
• Download Thread
• Upload Thread
• Daily Maintenance Thread

More sophisticated programs are often *multi-threaded*. Typically, the main procedure controls the user interface, and "worker threads" are started to perform time-consuming operations in the background such as file downloads or long-running calculations.

An application can also create threads that exist for the entire life of the application. In the sidebar here, for example, the *database thread* might be started when the application is initialized. The main thread can post a message to the database thread when it wants to access the database, and the database thread can notify the main thread via an *event* or some shared data structure when the requested information has been delivered from the database server back to the application.

On a simple processor the operating system schedules thread execution. Applications designed for multi-threading will perform better, and will generally be more responsive than a single-threaded equivalent because they can respond to the keyboard, mouse, and touch screen while the heavy-lifting is done in the background.

On a single-core systems, threads share the processor. This means that while one thread is waiting for I/O, for example, another thread can do some computing. On multi-core processors such as you find in current PCs, tablets, and smartphones, threads can actually do computing simultaneously. Therefore, not only do multi-threaded applications run better, but the system can run multiple applications together more efficiently.

Multi-core / multi-thread operation at the hardware level is entirely transparent to an application. However, the drawback of threads at the software level is that they can be difficult to program. The "Unix-style" of creating a system is usually to create a number of simple applications (processes) that perform specific tasks. One application might create a generalized report that contains more information than you want. The generalized report can be passed along to another filtering application that selects only the portions you are interested in. This is usually a clean and flexible approach, but it is not the most efficient.

An equivalent solution can be created as a single process with multiple threads. In the Unix-style case, the two processes usually execute serially. In the multi-threaded case, the two steps can be executed mostly in parallel. However, the "detailed report thread" constantly needs to know if the "generalized report generator" thread has any new information to be filtered. Furthermore, the "main thread" needs to known when all of the worker threads have completed, which requires that all of the threads are somehow synchronized. Such an application structure can result in faster overall execution time, but if not coded properly can result in all kinds of problems such as Race Conditions as discussed later.

In summary, threads provide a way to maximize processor utilization by allowing an application to perform multiple tasks with minimal overhead. On the other hand, they are more complicated to program. Finally, "pro-process" people point out that if a thread fails there is a potential to bring down the entire application, whereas if a separate process is used, only that other process will fail. That is perhaps a valid suggestion for an application such as a web server, but the point of this book is to help make solid applications, so let's explore some more.

Types of Memory

Below are the buzz words used in relationship to kinds of memory in a computer system.

Table 4 - Types of Memory

Type	Description

Static	Memory that is allocated when a program starts, and exists for the entire duration of the program run. Examples of this include window and button titles that do not change at runtime. You can also have static items that do change at runtime such as the area where a name can be stored. The contents may change at runtime, but the space to store it is fixed for the duration of the run.
Global	This is exactly the same as Static memory, but with one subtle exception: Static memory variables are only "visible" within the procedure or file in which they are defined, whereas global variables are visible to the entire program. For example, an application might have hundreds of variables named "count" for use in counting things, and these would be Static (or Stack) variables (see below). You might also have "TheCustomerDataTable" that a number of routines need to use, and you only want a single instance of this data, so this could be a Global variable.
Stack	Static memory allocation is not an efficient way to use available memory. Why waste space on the hundreds of variables named "count", which are only used once in a while and only for a short time? To avoid wasted space, many programming languages allow you to create short-lived variables like these on the Stack.
	The Stack is a fixed area of memory, but access to it works like a stack of plates in a cafeteria. When a plate is placed on the stack, the stack automatically shifts down, and when someone takes a plate, the stack automatically shifts back up. The Stack is this spring-loaded plate holder, and each plate is analogous to a memory cell.
	When a procedure needs space for temporary variables *count, x, y*, and *z*, it can grab some of the space on the stack, and when done it just gives back the space. This is a very fast operation, and is a more efficient use of memory because stack space is reused over-and-over again.
	The Stack is also used for two other purposes. Procedures call other procedures. The *called* procedure needs to know how to get back to where it came from, and this information (the "*return*

	address") is stored on the Stack. Additionally, some procedures operate with *parameters*. For example, to use a "SquareRoot" function, you need to tell it the value for which you wish to calculate the root. *Arguments* (the actual value of the function's *parameters*) are passed on the Stack. Bad things can happen to applications that use the stack improperly, which I'll go into later.
Dynamic	There is another memory area referred to as "the heap", where memory can be allocated and the allocated objects are kept for the long term (not just for the duration of a procedure). For example, "TheCustomerDataTable" mentioned above might be allocated when the application starts, modified from time to time, and de-allocated when the application terminates. Whereas objects allocated on the Stack are typically rather small, objects in the heap can be any size up to some system limit. Problems that can occur with the heap are be discussed later.
Swap	Swap / Swapped / Swapping memory isn't actually a consideration during application design, but is mentioned here for completeness. The operating system loads an application into memory and runs it. If the system wants to run another application that won't fit into memory at the moment, some or all of the first application will be "swapped" (written) to disk so that the second application can be brought in. When the system wants to continue the first application, it swaps out some or all of the second application, and swaps the first application back in.
Virtual	Virtual Memory in general is not of much concern in the design of most applications, but again is included for completeness. Like swapping, the operating system manages the available physical memory, and creates something called a *page table* for each application that maps some "logical" chunk of the application's memory into a real "physical" chunk of memory in the machine. These chunks of memory are called "pages", and a

	page is typically 1KB to 8KB, depending on the CPU architecture. With swapping, the operating system needs to manage everything, but with virtual memory, the hardware assists by generating a "*page fault*" when the page that an application needs is not available (i.e., it is either still on disk, or was paged out to disk). At this point, the operating system catches the fault, throws out pages that have not been used recently, and then loads required page. A case where an application uses virtual memory directly is when handling "memory mapped files". This technique allows you to open a file and have the operating system map it into your application's memory space. The application can then treat the file as an in-memory data structure as opposed to a binary or text file, which can sometimes be convenient depending on the application design. Both Swapping and Virtual Memory allow you to run more applications that can actually fit into memory at once. Adding physical memory will almost always speed up a system because the system can keep more pages in memory, and accessing memory is much faster than accessing a disk.
ROM	Read-Only Memory. Memory for storing a fixed program. ROM usually refers to "masked ROM" where the program is written inside the chip at production time. A ROM is application-specific, and cannot be changed.
PROM	Programmable ROM. This can refer to ROM, and can also refer to a special kind of ROM that can be programmed exactly once from outside the chip. A PROM is more general than a ROM, and can be used for any kind of application.
EPROM	Erasable PROM. PROM that can be erased in the field using ultraviolet light, and then reprogrammed with an "EPROM Programming" machine.
EEPROM	Electrically Erasable PROM. A PROM that can be reprogrammed electrically anywhere from 10,000 to 1,000,000 times depending on the technology used. Many computers use EEPROM to store configuration information; many microprocessors have a small

	amount of EEPROM built-in.
FLASH	A variation of EEPROM, but with faster access time. Due to its low cost and speed advantage, FLASH memory is popular in portable storage devices such as "USB Thumb Drives".

Memory-Related Bugs: Quick Explanation

If a program does not follow all of the rules of working with memory, some very bad things can happen. A few examples are:

- NULL Pointer Dereference. Accessing data through an incorrectly initialized pointer normally causes a program to abort with an "Access Violation" (Windows") or "Segmentation Fault" (Linux).
- Dangling Pointer Dereference. Using a pointer that no longer refers to the original data can cause either a crash or data corruption.
- Memory Leak. Failure to free dynamically allocated memory after use means that you'll probably keep chewing up more and more memory until you eventually run out. This can bring both the application and the system to its knees.
- Buffer Overflow / Array Out-of-Bounds. If you accidentally try to access memory outside of an object's allocated bounds, you can easily cause inexplicable behavior including destroying unrelated data objects.

Memory-related problems are, unfortunately, very easy to create by mistake, will make an application fail in mysterious ways, and are very difficult to debug.

In the list of languages previously mentioned you may have noticed C# and Java. Both of these languages are similar to C++, but they basically take away pointer handling from you, and deallocation of dynamically allocated memory is handled through "*automatic garbage collection*".

At this point you should absolutely be wondering: If "C" and C++ can be so troublesome, why on earth should we use them? The answer is actually very simple: Java, C#, and Visual Basic are for creating go-carts. A go-cart is cute, goes fast enough for most people, and you don't even need a license to drive one. "C" and C++ are for making rocket-powered sports cars (your mission critical software), where speed and stability are everything, and cuteness is probably not even an issue.

Most end-user applications (e.g., "reservation entry") are go-carts. The database server hidden in the back room, however, has to process thousands of reservation per second and needs to be a nitromethane-powered dragster driven by a clever "C"or C++ program. Similarly, the Powertrain Control Module (sometimes known as the Engine Control unit) needs to be inexpensive, work perfectly, *and* stop when you say stop, not when the garbage collection routine feels like it. It does not need cute things like user-definable emoticons, and there aren't hundreds of megabytes of free space to store the .Net Framework or Java runtime.

Finally, I should mention C++ "Smart Pointers". These provide a mechanism to automatically free dynamically allocated memory when the associated pointer goes out of scope, and are becoming popular in new applications as they become more standardized.

Other Types of Bug: Quick Explanation

The problems mentioned previously are specific to languages such as "C" and C++ that allow dynamic memory allocation. Problems that can occur in *all* languages are as follows:

- Numeric overflow or underflow.
- Division by zero. In most systems this will cause the application to terminate.
- Out-of-bounds access to an array.
- Uninitialized variables.

Chapter Summary

This chapter introduced some basic Computer Science concepts, and introduced terminology that will be used in the detailed discussion of bugs.

Chapter 3: Creepy Bugs

This chapter describes categories of bugs that commonly occur, are generally difficult to detect, and can also have a devastating impact on an application. In particular, you will learn how to detect and correct Array Bounds, Buffer Overflow, Deadlock, Memory Leaks, Race Conditions, Resource Leaks, and other kinds of complex software bugs that can bring an application or system to its knees.

In the words of Brian Kernighan, *"Debugging is twice as hard as writing the code in the first place. Therefore, if you write code as cleverly as possible, you are, by definition, not smart enough to debug it."*[1]

While this implies that you ought to have complete morons writing code and leave debugging up to your brightest stars, the situation isn't really that dire. Programming itself isn't all that fun. Just know that when you see a programmer in a state of euphoria, it is because he or she just figured out a hard bug. The fun is in doing all of the detective work.

This chapter is primarily for developers, but managers are encouraged to skim it, or read about particular bugs in detail when such a case arises.

Plain Old Logic Errors

This category covers any case where the program does not do what was intended. They can be caused by:

- Ambiguous Specifications, which is almost always the case!
- Changing Specifications. This is also almost always the case.

- Information Overload or not enough time to understand it. A case in point is the specification for Microsoft's Xml Document format, which is about 6,000 pages long. Microsoft was certainly "safe" in opening this specification to the public—there are only a few people on the planet who would want to try to implement a clone application.
- Unknown or Impossible Goal. The specification may require using the software or hardware in new and mysterious ways that may or may not be possible to do.
- Typographical errors.
- Too many interruptions from the boss, other staff, or customers.
- Time-to-market pressure.

Plain Old Logic Errors are usually obvious, so they are usually caught during initial testing. They are not as "creepy" as the bugs described in detail in the rest of this chapter.

Allocation/Deallocation Mismatch

Symptoms: Memory Leak. Inexplicable behavior.

In "C", objects are allocated by one of the malloc()-related runtime functions, and released with the free() function. In C++, simple objects can be allocated and released the same way, but usually you use the *new* and *delete* operators. In addition to allocation and deallocation, these operations will also execute a *constructor* that contains extra initialization code, and a *destructor* that contains extra cleanup code.

It is important that objects are created and destroyed using the correct pair of operations (malloc() and free(), or new and delete). Otherwise, anomalous behavior will occur.

In C++, there is also a common error in allocating and releases arrays. For example:

```
char* pMyString = new char[100];
...
delete pMyString; // Should be delete [] pMyString!
```

Here I've allocated an array of 100 bytes. However, the array operator "[]" was omitted from the delete statement, so the entire array is not deleted. The opposite case can occur where you accidently say "delete []" for something that is not an array.

Detection and Correction

Compilers are not very good at detecting this, even within the same function, never mind across functions or files. Your best bet is therefore trying to catch these with a good Static Analysis tool that can perform inter-procedural checks of this type. Some Dynamic Analysis tools may be able to catch these as mismatches, but they are likely to report an incomplete array deletion as a Memory Leak.

Arithmetic Problems (Integer)

Symptoms: Application or system crash. *Inexplicable* behavior, particularly incorrect results. Data loss.

This section discusses overflow and underflow problems for integer arithmetic. For problems with floating point numbers refer to <u>Floating Point Problems</u>.

NOTE: Most of the arithmetic problems described in this section also fall under the category of "Undefined Behavior". The C/C++ specifications do not state what is supposed to happen when you do some of the funny things in these examples. Therefore, the examples show what you are *likely* to see.

Integer (whole number) arithmetic is completely accurate provided that you don't exceed the limits of the machine architecture as shown below.

Table 5 - Integer Ranges

Size in Bits	Signed Range	Unsigned Range
8	-128 to +127	0 to 255
16	-32,768 to +32,767	0 to 65,535
32	-2,147,483,648 to 2,147,483,647	0 to 4,294,967,295
64	-9,223,372,036,854,775,808 to 9,223,372,036,854,775,807	0 to 18,446,744,073,709,551,615

In *two's complement arithmetic*, 1 bit of the value is used for the sign (0 means positive, 1 means negative), and the remaining bits contain the value. With this scheme, the range of signed values then becomes -2^{n-1} through $+2^{n-1} - 1$, where "n" is the number bits that can be accessed at once, for example, 32. There is also *one's complement* arithmetic, but it is used only in odd-ball or ancient devices.

With two's complement arithmetic, if you add 1 to a 32-bit signed integer with a value of 2147483647 ("INT_MAX", the maximum value that will fit in 31 bits) you end up with the value -2147483648 ("INT_MIN"). Wrap-around occurs because the digits overflow into the *sign bit*. And, by the way, the internal bit pattern in this case happens to look suspiciously like *"minus zero"* (80000000 in hexadecimal).

Similarly, multiply two small 16-bit numbers such as 10 x 20, and the result is, thankfully, 200. Change this to 30000 x 10 and the result becomes 10,176! This is because the maximum theoretical value you can get by multiplying two 16-bit values can be 32-bits long (including the sign), but the 16-bit multiply only saves the lower 16-bits.

Another corner case is when you divide INT_MIN by -1. The result is INT_MIN (the sign does not change).

Most of the time, the results are going to cause a problem. For example:

- Your pizza comes out of your digital toaster oven either undercooked or burnt to a crisp. Not too serious, and you learn to live it by adjusting the timer.
- A code loop that is performing a repeated calculation will run an incorrect number of times.
- An array index is calculated incorrectly, resulting in selecting the wrong array element, or worse, the program crashes.
- You over or under-compensate on the stepping motor that you are controlling. Serious problem if you are controlling the flaps on a jet airplane.

- A hacker might be able to alter program behavior or access secure data by creating bogus application states that the application designer did not anticipate.

  A very dangerous case is where overflow results while calculating a buffer size. If the allocated buffer size is too small, subsequent code may cause a buffer overrun. When memory surrounding the overflowed buffer has been corrupted, the entire application can become unstable, and possibly insecure.

Unsigned integers by definition wrap around on overflow. Many programs are coded to use this to their advantage. For example, on Windows you can use GetTickCount() to calculate elapsed time in milliseconds. Even though the "ticks" counter can overflow, the subtraction works correctly up to a total elapsed time of approximately 48 days. However, you can still get into trouble if an unsigned loop counter overflows.

Detection and Correction

Unfortunately, integer overflow detection capability is nothing less than depressing. Very few Static or Dynamic Analysis tools can actually detect this kind of problem correctly and efficiently.

Therefore, options for dealing with this are:

- Range-check the values you are working with before using them.
- Code in assembler language so you can test the processor's overflow flag.
- Use a "smart integer library" that can return an error when overflow has occurred.

- Use techniques such as shown below (which could be implemented in a "smart integer library".)

One technique for detecting potential overflow is described in Robert Seacord's book[2] and at www.securecoding.cert.org. For addition:

```
/* Two's complement case */
signed int si1, si2, sum;
/* Initialize si1 and si2 */
if ( ((si1^si2) | (((si1^(~(si1^si2) & INT_MIN)) + si2)^si2)) >= 0) {
    /* handle error condition */
}
else {
    sum = si1 + si2;
}

/* General case */
signed int si1, si2, sum;
/* Initialize si1 and si2 */
if (((si2>0) && (si1 > (INT_MAX-si2)))
    || ((si2<0) && (si1 < (INT_MIN-si2)))) {
    /* handle error condition */
}
else {
    sum = si1 + si2;
}
```

A slightly more readable way of expressing the two's complement test above is:

```
if ((a > 0) && (b > INT_MAX - a)) {
    /* Would overflow... */
}
else if ((a < 0) && (b < INT_MIN - a)) {
    /* This would underflow, too... */
}
else {
    /* Do addition... */
}
```

The reason I find all of this depressing is because of the extra overhead involved. To avoid the overhead, it would be nice if the processor could generate a hardware exception, but there does not seem to be a consistent way of doing this between compilers or versions of the same compiler, never mind on different processors.

GNU offers the –ftrapv and –fwrapv command line options to deal with integer overflow. However, these options apparently do not work consistently, and I have personally yet to see them work. Microsoft C/C++ does not offer an equivalent option.

So, my advice is:

- For C++, use a library such as SafeInt. This is a set of templates for dealing with overflow. It is included in recent versions of Microsoft Visual C++.
- For C, the situation is a bit more dire. The "safe_iop" library (version 0.3) from Google Code compiles with GNU, but not with Microsoft C/C++. And, the "IntegerLib" library from CERT

(https://www.securecoding.cert.org) seems to have been deprecated already.

- Use assembler code such as that described below.
- For C#, use the "checked" keyword (e.g., "i = checked(j + k)" in critical pieces of code. This will throw an OverflowException on overflow.
- Java does not have a "checked" keyword as in C#. This means you will probably have to resort to adding safety checks similar to those shown above (under Seacord's method). For certain calculations, you may be able to use Java's BigInteger and BigDecimal arbitrary precision classes.

If you are willing to use assembler language, you can detect overflow with the code below. This will work on an x86 or x64_86 machine with either Microsoft Visual C/C++ or GNU and you can add additional code for other processors or compilers if required.

```
#define X86_OVERFLOW_FLAG 0x800
#ifdef __WIN32
/* NOTE: Enable Intrinsic Functions (/Oi) in
    the compiler optimization settings */
#define GetX86Flags __readeflags
#else  /* Assume GNU */
static inline __attribute__((always_inline))
unsigned short GetX86Flags() {
  unsigned short flags;
  asm __volatile__ (
    "pushfw\n\t"
    "popw %%ax"
    : "=a"(flags) : : "cc"
  );
  return flags;
}
#endif
```

To use this, you might then have code like this:

```
int i = INT_MAX;
i += 1;
if ((GetX86Flags() & X86_OVERFLOW_FLAG) != 0) {
    ...handle error...
}
```

For ARM architecture and ARM's "*armcc*" compiler you can look at the APSR register to get the condition codes including the overflow bit. This register has the interesting characteristic that its layout depends on the _endianness_ of the particular system, so you need to handle dual-layouts for the APSR register!

```
#ifdef __BIG_ENDIAN
typedef union {
    struct {
        int N:1;
        int Z:1;
        int C:1;
        int V:1;
        int Q:1;
        int _dnm:19;
        int I:1;
        int F:1;
        int T:1;
        int mode:5;
    } b;
    unsigned int word;
} PSR;
#else /* Little Endian (most systems) */
typedef union {
    struct {
        int mode:5;
        int T:1;
        int F:1;
        int I:1;
        int _dnm:19;
```

```
        int Q:1;
        int V:1;
        int C:1;
        int Z:1;
        int N:1;
      } b;
      unsigned int word;
    } PSR;
    #endif /* __BIG_ENDIAN */

    register PSR apsr __asm("apsr");
    ...test for overflow as required...
```

If you want to throw an exception after an overflow, you can call "RaiseException(EXCEPTION_INT_OVERFLOW, 0, 0, NULL);" on Windows, or raise(SIGFPE) on Linux. For Intel code, you unfortunately cannot use the INTO (INTerrupt on Overflow) instruction on an x64 machine, so you cannot embed smart overflow handling directly in the assembler code.

Furthermore, if you *do* want to throw an exception for integer overflow, it can only be done on statement-by-statement basis. You cannot, in general, enable these exceptions for the entire application such as you can usually do by setting flags for the floating point control unit.

Once you have detected an overflow, you then have these options as to how to deal with it:

- Ignore it.
- Report an error via an exception.
- Assert (abort).
- Saturate the result (set the result to the maximum or minimum allowable value).
- Reserve one value to represent "Not a Number".

Other Ways of Performing Calculations

Three other ways of performing arithmetic that come to mind are:

- Floating Point. This may be appropriate if you just need to deal with a larger range of values. However, remember that floating point has limited precision, so you can never use it where absolute precision is required.
- Fixed Point. Fixed Point (aka Decimal) arithmetic can provide extended precision compared to integer arithmetic. For example, in C# you can get 28 digits of precision using the System.Decimal data type. Unfortunately, Fixed Point arithmetic is not supported natively by C/C++. You may be able to use a library such as Libmpdec[3], or you can roll your own code without too much difficulty.
- Arbitrary-Precision Arithmetic. If you need to calculate ridiculous numbers such as the distance to Alpha Centauri in angstroms, you will have to use software-based arithmetic.

Array Bounds

Symptoms: Application or system crash. Inexplicable behavior.

An array is a collection of homogenous objects such as a set of characters containing a line of text, a table of sales totals indexed by day of the month, a collection of customer records, or a collection population figures indexed by latitude and longitude. An array is indexed by a *subscript* (or subscripts if multi-dimensional.)

Subscripts in C/C++ are zero-based, so the range is from 0 to the array size − 1. Using an out-of-bounds subscript will result in inexplicable behavior or a program crash.

Array subscripts are normally non-negative. However, in C/C++, arrays may also be accessed with pointers. For example, the following two lines are completely interchangeable:

```
x = List[i];
x = *(List + i);
```

Therefore, it is perfectly legal to have a pointer to somewhere in the array (up to 1 element beyond), and then access the array with something like "pointer[i]", where "i" can be negative. You can actually see this pattern in code generated by *yacc*, which uses a stack structure to store input tokens, and then it uses negative subscripts to access items lower on the stack.

Unrelated, there seems to be some confusion in the "C" standard in regards to the statement al"a pointer is valid to one item beyond the end of an array". The standard allows for this case:

```
char array[5];

char* p = array + 5;  // This is one beyond the end

while (*--p) {

    ...do something...

}
```

In this example, "p" starts out at one beyond the end of the array, and "p" is pre-decremented at the top of the while loop so it points to the actual ending element. The "C" standard does *not* imply that there is a magical extra memory cell that you can use. If you try to access one beyond the end (i.e., array[5]), you will be accessing some other object, or the program may simply fail. Furthermore, if you initialize "p" to *two* beyond the end of array but subtract *two* at the top of the loop, the code may work, but it is in violation of the "C" specification.

Detection and Correction

You probably will not find a subscript error until one has already caused a problem. If you cannot detect it easily in a debugger or by examining the code, try either a Dynamic or Static Analysis tool.

The best prevention is to code defensively, paying special attention to never trusting user input. Range check all input, and visually double-check your loop counters and parameters that are used to access arrays.

Buffer Overflow

🐛 *Symptoms*: Application or system crash. Inexplicable behavior.

A "buffer" is a temporary storage area in memory. For example, a block of raw data is read into a disk "buffer" before it is split into more human-oriented units such as lines and words. Buffering of data improves system performance by minimizing the number of times the application has to go into the operating system to fetch or store data from a storage device.

A "Buffer Overflow" occurs when the amount of data requested exceeds the amount of space allocated for it. If you try to store 100 characters in a variable that is only big enough to hold 20 characters, some very bad things can happen. Not only will the procedure return incorrect results, but if the overflow happens to wipe out the *return address*, the program can return to the *wrong place*. Hackers exploit this behavior by "returning" not to where they came from, but instead into some supposedly secure section of the program.

> Here's a cool one seen on an Internet forum:
>
> An application worked fine, except on Wednesdays in mid to late September.
>
> The buffer used to store a date string was too small to handle the worst case of "Wednesday" and "September".

A Buffer Overflow can be caused by:

- Simple miscalculation in determining the total the buffer size.

- Non-obvious typographical error.
- Failure to verify input parameters (not verifying somebody else's typing, and not taking a defensive stance against hackers).

Detection and Correction

The same advice that applies to Array Bounds also applies to Buffer Overflow problems, as well. Run a Static or Dynamic Analysis tool if possible. Double check your code to make sure you are passing the right parameters to functions, especially those that work with blocks of memory such as memcpy(), memmov(), and memset(). Never trust user input.

Dangerous Runtime Functions

🐛 *Symptoms*: Application or system crash. Inexplicable behavior. Data loss.

There are a number of functions built into the "C" language that are just plain dangerous to use. For compatibility reasons these functions cannot be removed, but you can avoid using them.

Table 6 - Dangerous "C" Runtime Functions

Function(s)	Vulnerability
atof(), atoi(), _atoi64(), atol(), _wtof(), wtoi(), _wtoi64(), _wtol()	These functions convert a number that is stored as a string to its internal numeric format (float, integer, or long). However, there is no way of reporting an error. Alternatives: strtol() and related functions are a slight improvement.
gets(), wgets()	These functions read an input line from the console, but are incapable of performing a bounds check. If the user inputs a line longer than the allocated buffer size, a buffer overflow will occur. Alternatives: fgets(), fgetws().
mktemp()	Return a unique, temporary file name. The generated file name was unique when the call was made, but another thread or process could have created a file by the same name by the time you try to create the file yourself. Alternatives: mkstemp().
strcat(), wstrcat(), mbscat()	These functions append one string to another. It is impossible to prevent buffer overflow.

	Alternatives: There are no standard alternatives. See strncat() below.
strncat(), wcsncat()	These functions append up to "n" characters to the destination. There is no parameter to indicate the size of the destination. Alternatives: There are no standard alternatives. However, strncat() is safer than strcat() if you calculate the source length such that it considers the current length of the destination area.
strcpy(), wcscpy(), mbscpy()	These functions copy one string to another. It is impossible to prevent buffer overflow if the source string is longer than the destination area. Alternatives: There are no standard alternatives, although using strncpy() is a bit safer (see below).
strncpy(), wcsncpy(), mbsncpy()	These functions are an improvement over the strcpy() family because they will limit the number of characters copied. However, if the output buffer is filled, strncpy() does not store a trailing null (0) character. The destination string will then appear to be merged with the memory directly above it, resulting in inexplicable behavior elsewhere. Alternatives: There are no standard alternatives. If you use this, always store a null character at the end of the array in case the destination area was filled up.
scanf(), wscanf()	These functions parse an input stream into sub-items such as integers and strings. However, input can overflow the assigned buffer space. Also, there is no way to detect numeric overflow. Alternatives: There are no standard alternatives. To prevent buffer

	overflows, specify length limits in the format strings, and range check the resulting numeric input.
sprint(), wprintf(), vsprintf(), vswprintf()	These functions create a formatted string. It is impossible to prevent buffer overflow. Alternatives: Use the alternative forms such as snprintf() and wnprintf().
strtok(), wcstok()	These functions split a string into tokens, and are frequently used in command line processing. Some implementations of these functions may not be thread-safe. For Microsoft C/C++, strtok() is thread-safe. For GNU you can use strtok_r(). For portability you therefore have to use a macro.
tempnam()	Return a unique, temporary file name. The generated file name was unique when the call was made, but another thread or process could have created a file by the same name by the time you try to create the file yourself. Alternatives: tmpfile().
>> input operator	The C++ input operator ">>" does not perform any bounds checking for character buffers.
Numerous Microsoft-specific functions with names similar to above such as lstrcpy(), lstrcat(), etc.	These functions are built into the Windows runtime, and are similar, including the dangers, to the equivalent functions that are in the "C" runtime.
Various	Check https://buildsecurityin.us-cert.gov/bsi/home.html for a list of other potential security pitfalls.

Note that Microsoft provides many functions that begin with "_t" that provide functionality similar to the functions listed in the previous table, for example, "_tcscpy()" works like strcpy(). This is actually a macro that allows the code to be built for use with either ANSI or Unicode characters, so the macro expands to either strcpy() or wcscpy() depending on the build options.

Detection and Correction

Modern compilers and some Static Analysis tools can report warnings when you use some of these functions. Specifically:

- Microsoft C/C++ from version 14.00 (Visual Studio 2005) by default will display warnings when a large subset of the functions in the above list are used.

  If you are *absolutely certain* that your code is safe, you can disable the warnings by defining the following:

  ```
  #define _CRT_SECURE_NO_DEPRECATE
  #define _CRT_SECURE_NO_WARNINGS
  #define _CRT_NON_CONFORMING_SWPRINTFS
  ```

- GNU compilers since 4.1 can generate link-time warnings when you use a dangerous function. However, the number of cases is extremely limited, making this feature not very valuable.

  Also, since GNU 4.0 and glibc 2.3.4 you can compile with −D_FORTIFY_SOURCE=n, where "n" is 1 for basic checks (the default), or "2" for additional checks. When optimization is then set to −O1 or higher, a few additional compile-time errors will be generated, and some additional runtime checking is performed on a subset of the dangerous functions. A documented caveat is that a value of 2 for "n" may break some programs.

- Search the source code for these functions, and replace with a safe alternative. If you are concerned about portability, unfortunately you will need to write your own "safe" equivalents.

Dangling Pointer Dereference

Symptoms: Application or system crash. Inexplicable behavior. Data loss.

Referencing a pointer or variable simply means reading or writing the variable. The following statement that touches a pointer variable will never do anything bad:

```
CUST_RECORD* pCustRecord = FindCustomer(CustomerID);
...
pCustRecord = // Invalid address, but this is not a dereference..
    (CUST_RECORD*)0xFFFFFFFF;
```

In a probable implementation of "FindCustomer()", the function will return the memory address of the customer record if found, or the special value "NULL" if not found. (NULL is "0" on most machines.)

Applications should always check that pointers they receive are valid before they are _dereferenced_, that is, before you try to access that memory that the pointer actually points to. Accessing the "NULL" pointer is a special case that can cause problems as described under "NULL Pointer Dereference".

A Dangling Pointer Deference occurs when a once valid pointer is dereferenced. For example, suppose we now do this:

```
CUST_RECORD* pCustRecord = FindCustomer(CustomerID);
if (pCustRecord != NULL) {
  pCustRecord->Balance = 0;
  delete pCustRecord;  // CustomerRecord is now invalid
  pCustRecord->ClosedDate = GetCurrentDate();
}
```

By definition in C/C++, once a memory object has been "freed" or "deleted" ("pCustRecord" above), any pointers to it are invalid, and you must never dereference those pointers again until they are reset to point to other proper data. The pointer variables themselves still exist, but they are "dangling", pointing at who knows what. They are also dangling in front of the eyes of the developer, tempting the developer to do dangerous things with them.

If you use a Static Analysis tool, the particular case above may be reported either a "Dangling Dereference" error or a "Use After Free" error.

At runtime, the following bad things can occur:

- On a high-end processor, a fault can be generated, and the user may receive an "Access Violation" error on Windows, or a "Segmentation Fault" on Linux. This is unlikely, though, because the pointer *probably* still refers to an area of memory still accessible by the current process.
- The application may continue, but something important may have been destroyed, making the application do bizarre things later on. The worst case is in a multi-threaded application where one thread uses memory that it no longer owns. First of all, this thread is not handling its own data correctly. Secondly, a different thread may now be reusing the same memory for a different purpose, and the first thread could be overwriting good data with nonsensical data.

Dangling Pointer Dereferences are likely to occur when a procedure is long and complex, therefore making it difficult to see the whole picture. (Any procedure that will not fit in your field of vision is probably not a good piece of code, although exceptions are allowed for cases that are clearly unavoidable.)

A less obvious way that these can occur is when using source code editors that offer "code completion", which is somewhat like "auto-correct" in a word processor. You can tear out a lot of hair during debugging, until you realize that you are not even using the variable that you intended to use.

Detection and Correction

Dangling Pointer Dereferences are very difficult to spot by eye. A Static Analysis tool can be used to automate the search.

A common trick that some people use is to define a macro such as "SAFE_FREE(ptr)". This macro can call free(), and then set "ptr" to NULL. This does not fix a incorrect dereference problems. Instead, it will cause a NULL Dereference error to occur, which is easier to pick up while debugging.

To fix these problems in the source code, some heavy restructuring of the code may be required to avoid the use of the offending pointer(s).

Dead Code and Unreachable Code

 Symptoms: Wasted memory, Inexplicable behavior.

"Dead" is code that calculates something, but the result is never used. Dead code is often the artifacts remaining after a modification. Occasionally, Dead Code may cause another problem such as Divide by Zero.

"Unreachable" Code is code that cannot possible ever execute. For example:

```
if (FALSE) {
    ...cannot reach this code...
}
```

Since this code can never execute, it is just wasting memory. Furthermore, this is potentially a bug because the programmer probably meant to type something else such as "if (Result == FALSE) ...", in which case the application can exhibit inexplicable behavior.

Some coding standards require that you do not have any Dead or Unreachable code.

Detection and Correction
Modern compilers can usually detect Dead Code, and will display a warning that "such-and-such a variable is unused." They can also detect Unreachable Code if the conditional expression is known at compile time (i.e., the expression is a constant).

Static Analyzers can usually detect Dead Code, and can sometimes detect Unreachable Code cases where there this is no combination of parameters that would allow a conditional expression to be true.

To fix Dead Code, simply delete it.

To fix Unreachable Code, adjust the conditional expression as required.

Deadlock

 Symptoms: Application or system hang up.

Processes and threads sometimes need to access objects that are shared with other threads. Access to shared objects must be made *mutually exclusive*. In other words, two processes or threads may not modify the same object at the same time.

A deadlock occurs when the following conditions occur:

- Processes or threads incrementally request exclusive access to resources and then hold on to those resources.
- Resource ownership may not be preempted.
- Ownership is circular—one thread or process is waiting for a resource owned by another thread or process.

> Deadlock (Circular Ownership Problem):
>
> Me: "Honey, I forgot my commuter pass. Can you come pick me up?"
>
> Wife: "Sure [stupid]. Where are the car keys?"
>
> Me: "In my pocket."

Operating systems and processors provide a number of mechanisms to implement mutual exclusion, or *atomic access*. Common types of mutual exclusion "locking" mechanisms are shown in the following table.

Table 7 - Mutual Exclusion Methods

Type	Description
Critical Section	High-performance, reentrant. Windows-only.
Mutex	Mutual exclusion object. Reentrant. Windows, POSIX threads (Linux, Mac OS, others).
Semaphore	A "resource dealer" that doles out resources as long as they are available, otherwise the requestor must wait. Not reentrant. Windows, POSIX.
Spin Lock	Fast, but heavy overhead if the lock has already been acquired by another thread. In a simple implementation, the requestor sets a flag, and if the flag was already clear it proceeds. If the flag was already set, it "spins" in a tight loop repeating the test until the interrupt-driven owner of the lock releases it by clearing the flag. Used primarily in operating system code including device drivers.
Atomic Hardware Instruction	Some processors such as the Intel x86 family implement instructions such as "InterlockedExchange" that guarantee no other thread, process, or processor can access the same memory until the instruction completes. The Windows SDK provides supporting functions such as InterlockedIncrement(). GNU compilers support these operations with built-in functions such as _sync_add_and_fetch().

Some of the synchronization methods shown above are marked as "reentrant". These are methods where the owning thread can request the same resource multiple times without blocking. A thread that calls a non-reentrant lock multiple times will cause itself to hang forever.

In addition to the synchronization methods mentioned above, modern operating systems also support some kind of an *event* signaling mechanism. This allows one thread or process to sleep until some condition occurs such as "data available". Setting an event object tells the operating system to wake up the sleeping thread.

C# and Java provide built-in support for synchronized access to shared objects, although it is the programmer's job to turn on this support where required. In C/C++, a bit more typing is involved, but it is not at all complicated.

In regards to bugs and shared data access, the danger is that if you do not use mutual exclusion objects, you risk causing all kinds of bizarre behavior when one thread trashes the data also being accessed by another thread.

However, when you introduce locking mechanism, you may also introduce Deadlocks, which will cause the program to hang.

Detection and Correction

At the coding level, Deadlocks can be caused by any of the following reasons:

- Failure to release a lock. This type of coding error is likely to show up early in the debug phase, provided that the particular code is exercised a lot.
- Incorrect locking or unlocking sequence, as described below.

There is a dearth of Static Analysis tools for analyzing Deadlock problems – because it is a difficult problem to address. Some Static Analysis tools can find simple Deadlock cases, but the tools that I have looked at primarily depend on heuristics. ("You locked 'xyz' over there; shouldn't you lock it here, too?")

Some Dynamic Analysis tools can detect Deadlocks. The only problem is that with a Dynamic Analysis tool, you must actually exercise the code in order for a bug to be detected. Additionally, the bug may be dependent on timing or input data.

Lacking good detection tools, the best prevention is therefore a good design. The number of places where locks occur is likely to be limited to a handful of routines, so careful study of the code ought to be feasible. The basic coding rules are:

- For simple multi-threaded applications, use only a single lock. This avoids lock ordering problems. However, this may not be a good solution for more sophisticated applications because it may limit multi-threaded performance.

- If multiple locks are required, establish a locking sequence where resources are always locked and unlocked in the same order. This order may *not* necessarily be the same as the order in which you want to *use* the objects, but strictly adhering to this practice will avoid problems when objects are locked incrementally.

  You can assign a numeric level to various locks and include this in the name of the lock as a visual hint.

Then, to avoid circular ownership problems, always lock in the same order, and never request a lock at a lower level than what you already own.

- Where practical, lock all objects at once; give up if you cannot lock all of the objects that you need.

Divide by Zero (Integer)

 Symptoms: Application or system crash.

On most systems, division by zero will cause the application to abort. Most programs avoid this with a simple test for the divisor being zero.

Detection and Correction

To avoid Divide by Zero errors, test that the divisor is non-zero. That is the easy part. You may also need to redesign the flow to account for where you avoid the error case.

To find potential trouble spots:

- Use a Static Analysis tool, especially if the program does a lot of math.
- If the application does not perform a lot of math *and* the code is nicely formatted with spaces surrounding the "/" (division) operator, it is easy to search for possible error cases. If there are no spaces surround the "/", you have a nightmare, of course, because "/" are also part of C/C++ comments.

Documentation Error

Beat on your suppliers and your staff as well to provide adequate and correct documentation.

There is nothing more frustrating than writing a lot of code that doesn't work, and then you find out that the instructions were wrong in the first place. So you have wasted a huge amount of time looking for a non-existent bug—at least in your own code.

How's this sentence that describes some hardware options:

"Add a jumper between pins 1 and 8, or pins 2 and 6."

This looks harmless enough, and at first glance it seems like you have a choice of where to add the jumper. We tried both cases without success, so we then spent a huge amount of time staring at our new driver code.

Electrically, a jumper wire performs a logical "OR" function. The correct English (which I figured out on a whim) should have been something like:

"Add a jumper between pins 1 and 8, <u>and also</u> add a jumper between pins 2 and 6."

Adding two OR jumpers finally fixed the problem.

Also beware of any explanations of error handling. Did the authors actually test the extreme cases? I have some code that has to do some extreme things when an extremely unlikely event happens, and it is nearly impossible to purposely trigger the event. Guess what? It does happen about once every 15 years, and it happened on a very important client's system. Worse, the recovery logic did not work as I had hoped.

I don't know if there is a lesson in here, other than "don't trust anybody."

Sorry, I just wanted to get this out of my system.

Endianness

Symptoms: Application or system crash. Incorrect results.

The word "endian" comes from Jonathan Swift's "Gulliver's Travels", where Lilliputins were required to break their eggs at the small end, while Blefuscuans were required to break their eggs at the big end. Basically, who cares? But, this was the official protocol in those two mythical places.

In a computer, the hardware designer has an option of how to store integer values, for example. If you have 32-bit integer, you can order the bytes of the value "1" in "little endian" format as on an Intel CPU like this:

01 00 00 00

> Pay attention at boring meetings!
>
> I was not really listening once during a presentation that I knew by heart. This was followed by questions in Japanese at Mach 2.4. One question was "Do you handle endianness?", and everybody in the room turned to me.
>
> It took me a few seconds before I realized that the word was English (strange as it may be).

Or, you can order the bytes in "big endian" format as on a Motorola CPU like this:

00 00 00 01

The little endian value could be misinterpreted on a big endian machine as 16,777,216. (Such an accidental bank deposit would be nice, but the bank would figure it out sooner or later.)

Endianness does not affect a high-level language such as C— unless you happen to be transmitting your data to systems of a different endianness—then you have to be very careful.

Endianness is an issue in these kinds of applications:

- The entire Internet! There are zillions of messages sent every day between devices of different endianness.
- Internal networks. Data is exchanged between PCs, tablets, smartphones, and servers.
- Automobiles. An automobile can have more than 100 processors. The most powerful ones are in the Powertrain Control Module, transmission, and the Navigation/Entertainment system. The processors can come from a number of manufacturers, and the designers of these processors all had different preferences for how to eat their eggs. However, the processors all have to talk to one another via various in-car networks such as Controller Area Network (CAN) and Local Interconnect Network (LIN).

Detection and Correction

Endianness is clearly a problem in critical automotive, aerospace, and communications applications. It is also a difficulty in consumer applications such as a web browser designed to run on multiple architectures.

Unfortunately, there is no straightforward way of dealing with this, other than to read the interface specifications and to be very careful while coding, especially in areas that deal with binary data that originates in another system.

If you examine any documentation related to TCP/IP, you will see that various packet fields are describes as being in "network byte order", which happens to be Big Endian. Your code typically stores data in these fields using the htonl() and htons(), and fetches data using ntohl() and ntohs(). These macros or functions convert long or short fields from host-to-network or network-to-host format. Conceptually, the same macros can be used for non-TCP/IP applications.

Floating Point Problems

 Symptoms: Incorrect results.

Floating Point (or "real numbers") are the continuous set of numbers in the range from −infinity to +infinity, for example, 1.0, 1.1, 1.11, 1.111, ..., 1.9999, ... , 1.2.

A computer can only approximately represent real numbers. For example, 1/3 as a real number repeats infinitely in a "0.3333", so the internal representation is close enough for many kinds of work, but is not exact.

Most computers use the IEEE-754[4] standard for storing floating point numbers. Ranges are:

Table 8 - IEEE-754 Floating Point Ranges

Type	Approximate Decimal Range
Single Precision (32-bit "float")	± ~10^{-44} to ~10^{38}.
Double Precision (64-bit "double")	± ~10^{-323} to ~10^{308}.
Double Precision Extended ("long double")	Implementation dependent. On an x86 with 80-bits, approximately ± $10^{\pm4932}$.

Floating point numbers are used primarily in engineering, scientific, and graphics applications. They are entirely useless for any kind of price calculations other than for estimates.

As with integer arithmetic, you must be careful about overflow, underflow, and division by zero. Although Integer Division by Zero would cause a runtime error, behavior of floating point errors can be set to be either "signaling" or "non-signaling". In the signaling case, an error will generate an exception. In the non-signaling case, computation continues, but you can test at the end of a loop whether the result came out to be a NaN (Not a Number), or Infinity.

Floating point errors can be trapped. Refer to "Unhandled Exception (Hardware)" and "Chapter 10: Debugging Tips".

And here's a weird one: IEEE-754 has both negative and positive zero. This is not useful to most of us, but in some mathematical calculations it is useful to know you are approaching zero from either the negative or positive side.

Another place where you can get into trouble is when you compare floating point results for an exact value. While negative and positive zero can be compared without problem due to special handling in the hardware, testing other values for equality may not work because the two values may differ by a miniscule fraction. For this you need to test if the result is within an acceptable range. For example, it might be appropriate to test for an absolute difference with "fabs(result – desiredResult) <= epsilon". Or, you may want to test for some percentage difference.

> "Honey, can I have some money?"
>
> Good mood answer: "Sure, take positive zero."
>
> Bad mood answer: "No, I have negative zero!"

There is another potential problem known as "sub-normals", where a value is so small that it cannot be normalized and compared to another value properly.

Extended Double Precision values may be implemented with 80 bits of sign, significand, and exponent, but they may occupy as much as 128 bits of storage. This may present problems during data interchange, so be sure to check your specific system architecture to find out what you are working with.

If you are performing extensive floating point calculations, you should spend some time researching the subject in more detail. There are many discussions about the topic on the Internet.

Free Non-dynamic Memory

Symptoms: Application or system crash. Inexplicable behavior.

As mentioned earlier, dynamic memory is allocated using the malloc() family of runtime functions, or in C++ using the *new* operator. Memory is then freed using free() or the *delete* operator.

Code such as this has a problem:

```
void MyFunction()
{
    int i = 0;
    free(&i)
}
```

The object that is freed here was *not* allocated on the heap, and in this case is a local variable allocated on the stack.

Detection and Correction

This type of error is rare, but they can occur due to misunderstanding of an interface.

Testing will reveal the error—if you have sufficient tests to hit the error case. Therefore, applying a good Static Analysis tool is more effective in finding these.

The correction to these problems is simple: don't free or delete objects that were not dynamically allocated.

You can also do the following:

- Microsoft C/C++ will generate a runtime error when such code is detected. GNU will generate a stack dump with no explanation. Other runtimes may or may not generate a runtime error, and may continue execution but cause inexplicable behavior.

- Most Static Analysis and Dynamic Analysis tools can detect these errors.

Incorrect Method Invocation

Symptoms: Application or system crash. Inexplicable behavior.

This is a category of bugs where as far as the compiler is concerned you have called a procedure correctly, but according to the specification you are not actually using it correctly. This is more likely to happen in C++, C#, and Java than in C. For example, in Java you might type:

```
myString.Trim();
```

However, rather than trimming trailing and ending spaces in-place, this operation returns a completely new string object, so the correct code should be:

```
myNewString = myString.Trim();
```

Another common case is when using iterators with the Standard Template Library (STL). A very bad design feature of STL is that when you delete an item in a container, the iterator is no longer valid. (You would hope that the delete function would update the iterator so that it references the next valid item, but it does not.) You just have to get used to this behavior, and code accordingly—even if the code is not very efficient.

Detection and Correction

These kinds of errors are easy to introduce. Working in multiple languages, I forget all the time. And, as mentioned above, the compiler usually does not report an error.

Your best bet for detecting these is to run each newly coded procedure through a Static Analysis tool that can detect API misusage. Some Static Analysis tools can detect specific kinds of misuse, and other tools can catch the case where you accidently ignored the return value of some function. You can also step through each new procedure with a debugger to verify that it behaves as expected. That's what I always do with new code anyway.

To correct these problems, refer to the API documentation.

Invalid Cast

🐛 *Symptoms*: Application or system crash. Inexplicable behavior.

A "cast" in "C" forces the compiler to convert one primitive data type to another. For example:

```
MyIntegerValue = 1.5;
```

This statement implicitly converts the double precision (real) value "1.5" to integer "1", truncating (chopping off) the fraction. With the compiler warning level set high enough, most compilers will also emit a warning message.

Programmers can and should, however, signify their intention to others who might read the source code, and to avoid warning messages. This can be done with a cast such as this:

```
MyIntegerValue = (int)MyRealValue;
```

In addition to the traditional "C" cast, C++ offers these variations:

- const_cast. Removes the *const* and *volatile* properties of an object. It is safe to use this when you have to coerce function parameters into another type. For example, your routine might have a parameter such as "const char* Filename"; you can use const_cast to pass this along to someone else's routine that expects "char* Filename". However, if an immutable object is actually modified the behavior is undefined.
- dynamic_cast. This type of cast is handy when using polymorphic classes, that is, objects derived from a common base that provide a largely identical

interface. For example, specialized classes of Apple, Orange, and Banana could be derived from the base class Fruits. Using "Runtime Type Information" and dynamic_cast, an application can test which kind of derived class it is currently dealing with and then access that object's particular properties and behavior.

- reinterpret_cast. This type of cast is a little strange. The cast value is essentially a binary copy of the value being cast. Since the internal representation of a pointer is largely machine-specific, this type of cast should be limited to machine-specific code such as a device driver. In other words, you should use another type of cast unless you know exactly what you are doing.

- static_cast. This can be used as the equivalent of a "C" cast. It also allows conversion between base and derived classes. A static_cast does not have the overhead of a dynamic_cast, but the programmer is responsible for ensuring that requested conversions are valid.

Memory Leak

🐞 *Symptoms*: Application or system crash. Performance degradation.

A short-lived application that only runs for a few minutes or hours at a time can survive small memory leaks because modern operating systems including Windows, Linux, iOS, and Mac OS will free all of the memory used when the application exits.

Small memory leaks become a problem in long-lived applications such as a server system that runs continuously. Moderate or large memory leaks can also be a problem in short-lived applications such as a smartphone application that manipulates photographs. Photographic images may be several megabytes in size, and since the operating system wants to limit applications to perhaps 40MB maximum, leaking a few megabytes here and there quickly add up.

The most common understanding of Memory Leak is that some memory was allocated, but never freed. For example:

```
void ThisFunctionLeaksMemory()
{
        char* p;
        p = (char*) malloc(100);
}
```

Calling this function will probably not kill the application or the system. But, suppose this is a server application and this function is called frequently by client applications. Sooner or later, the server will get lethargic because there isn't enough free memory available. Without enough memory, the system starts "trashing" because it has to swap applications in and out of memory so frequently that effectively nothing gets done. Eventually, something will fail, and you might have hundreds of call center agents or dozens of equity traders who can't work for 15 minutes while the system is being reset.

On the technical side, let's generalize "forgot to free something", and consider this example, where we assume that whoever calls "GetListOfThings" is responsible for deleting the list when done:

```
ListItem* GetListOfThings()
{
                ...
        ListItem1 = new ListItem;
        ListeItem2 = new ListItem;
        ListItem1->NextItem = ListItem2;
        ListItem3 = new ListItem;
        ListItem2->Next = ListItem3;
                ...
        ListItem2->Next = NULL; // Bug!
                ...
        return ListItem1;
}
```

Notice near the end that the link between ListItem2 and ListItem3 is severed, and then the function returns. ListItem3 has become *unreachable* because no other code even knows of its existence, so obviously no code can possibly free it.

Therefore, the definition of Memory Leak should be "a situation where it is impossible to free dynamically allocated memory".

Detection and Correction

The first problem is that you have to discover that you have a memory leak. If you are lucky, the debug version of the runtime library will report memory leaks when your application exits.

You can also usually find memory leaks using a Dynamic Analysis tool. And, Static Analysis tools can find memory leaks, but the how well it can do this depends a lot on the quality of the tool, and whether or not the tool can do inter-procedural analysis.

If you need to manipulate complex data structures such as linked lists, queues, and hash tables, use library code whenever possible to avoid leaks and other bugs. There is no point in reinventing the wheel, and hopefully the library has hopefully already been debugged. For C++, look at the Standard Template Library ("STL") or Boost. For "C" you may be able to use the GNOME Library, "GLib".

For some compiler-specific tips on locating memory leaks, refer to "Chapter 10: Debugging Tips".

Realloc Memory Leaks

A fairly common cause of memory leaks is through misuse of the *realloc*() runtime function. Fortunately, these are easy to detect and easy to fix.

First, search for all occurrences of "realloc". Then look for instances like this:

```
char* SomePointer = (char*)realloc(SomePointer, NewSize);
```

The problem is that if realloc() *fails* it returns a value of NULL and leaves the original memory intact. However, this incorrect coding pattern wipes out the original pointer ("SomePointer"), thus making the memory unreachable and therefore leaked.

The correct pattern is like this:

```
char* SomeNewPointer = (char*)realloc(SomePointer, NewSize);
if (SomeNewPointer == NULL) {
    ...handle the error...
}
else {
    // Success, now save adjusted pointer
    SomePointer = SomeNewPointer;
    ...
}
```

False Memory Leaks

A tricky Memory Leak to deal with is a *false* Memory Leak. Occasionally, your debugger may report a leak at exit time. This happened to me once, and drove me crazy for several days. It turned out that sometimes there was still one thread that had requested to exit, but the exit had not really been processed by the operating system yet. When the main thread went through the "C" cleanup code, the "C" runtime code would then complain of a leak.

Fortunately, the operating system (Windows) will clean up all of the memory used by a process, so I finally decided that I could ignore the warning. Unfortunately, it means that I now always have to read the final messages from the runtime system to make sure I have not introduced a different leak.

Missing Return Value

Symptoms: Application or system crash. Inexplicable behavior. Incorrect results.

A C/C++ function that does not return a value is declared with a return type of "void". For example:

```
void SomeUtillityFunction()
{
        ...
}
```

Other functions typically return a value to be used in subsequent logic such as a customer record, a handle to a file that was opened, or an error code. For example:

```
int LoadConfiguration(const char* pszFileName)
{
    int ReturnCode = 0;
        ...
    if (some_condition)
        return; // Wrong!  Missing return value!
    ...
    return ReturnCode;  // Correct.
}
```

If a function with a non-void return type does not return a value matching the function's declared type, the compiler (unless it is ancient) should issue a warning—which should *not* be ignored, because the return value of the function will become whatever garbage happens to be hanging around when the function exits.

Detection and Correction

To correct these, you obviously need to fix the *return* statements in question so that they return an appropriate value.

Additionally:

- Many Static Analysis tools can detect this situation.
- The compiler can also probably detect this, but you need to enable warning messages and pay attention to them.

NULL Pointer Dereference

 Symptoms: Application or system crash.

For most hardware, lower memory addresses are typically reserved for special operations such as interrupt handling. Since location 0 is typically unusable by user-mode application, a symbol called NULL in C/C++ is defined via a macro to be "0". A pointer value set to NULL means to the application "I do not have any data corresponding to this pointer at this time." The C++ 2011 standard introduced a new keyword named "null" that eliminates a few odd problems of defining NULL as a macro.

Some computer veterans might remember some interesting machines such as from PR1ME Computer, where NULL was *not* 0. So people who code their NULL tests like this:

```
if (!MyPointer) {
   ...
}
```

would be in for a rude awakening when porting code to some old or weird machines. There is also a small amount of ambiguity in the language standards, so the only safe way to code this is:

```
if (MyPointer != NULL) {
   ...
}
```

Anyway, application programs are supposed to test pointer values that they receive before the pointer is dereferenced (i.e., before you try to access the object pointed to by the pointer). Failure to do so on a "real" processor normally results in an "Access Violation" (Windows), or a "Segmentation Fault" (Linux). Your toaster oven processor that does not have hardware memory protection will just go berserk.

There are two reasons why these errors can occur:

- The original developer knew in his heart that there is no way that some returned pointer will be NULL, so he or she omitted the safety check to save CPU cycles.
- The original developer was in a hurry and got tired of typing boring, extra lines of "if" statements.

What usually happens, though, is:

- The original developer didn't think of all the possible variations, and the missing safety check did not cover some extreme cases. For example, some code might work fine under normal circumstances—until the user unplugs the LAN cable.
- A new programmer comes along in a few months or years, doesn't know all of the assumptions that the original developer made, and manages to blow everything sky-high by using different assumptions.

Detection and Correction
To find these:

- A good Static Analysis tool will find places where pointer tests are missing.
- If you do not have a tool for finding these, Peer Review is another good way for helping to identify these weaknesses.

The solution for these problems is to add defensive code where required. It will take some time, and it will use a few extra CPU cycles. But, this defensive coding can prevent a catastrophe when someone modifies the code sometime later. You're excused from adding the safety checks only if you can prove that some returned pointer will *never* be NULL.

The fix to the source code usually involves changing one block of code into two blocks to handle the NULL and non-NULL cases. In a good case, you can fix this with a few minutes of editing.

There is a case that might not be as straightforward, though.

Suppose that the original code did not return an error code such as "out of memory". When the dual code blocks mentioned above are added, this may now introduce a problem in higher level code where the callers need to know if the modified routine succeeded or not. That means that dozens of calling routines may need to be modified to handle the failure case, and editing everything may turn out to be a big, but unavoidable chore.

Operator Precedence Misunderstanding

🐞 *Symptoms*: Inexplicable behavior.

Unless you have completely forgotten elementary school, you know that division is performed before multiplication, and multiplication is performed before addition and subtraction.

Besides basic arithmetic operators such as addition, subtraction, multiplication, and division, all programming languages have many more math and logical operators. Each operator has precedence (priority), but the precedence is not always what you would expect. The precedence table (highest to lowest) for C++ is shown below. "C" uses a subset of these operators.

Table 9 - C++ Operator Precedence

Precedence	Operator	Description	Associativity
1	::	Scope resolution.	None.
2	++ and --	Post-increment, and Post- decrement.	Left-to-right.
	()	Function call.	
	[]	Array subscript.	
	.	Select element by reference.	
	->	Select element by pointer.	
3	++ and --	Post-increment, and Post- decrement.	Right-to-left.
	+ and -	Unary plus and minus.	
	! and ~	Logical NOT and bitwise NOT.	
	(type)	Type cast.	
	*	Indirection (dereference a pointer).	
	&	Take address of object.	

	sizeof	Take compile-time size of object.	
	new	Allocate dynamic memory (C++).	
	delete	Free dynamic memory (C++).	
4	.* ->*	Pointer to member.	Left-to-right.
5	* / %	Multiplication, division, and remainder (modulo).	Left-to-right.
6	+ and -	Addition and subtraction.	Left-to-right.
7	<< and >>	Bitwise left and right shift.	Left-to-right.
8	< <= > and >=	Relational comparisons.	Left-to-right.
9	== and !=	Relational comparisons "equal" and "not equal".	Left-to-right.
10	&	Bitwise AND.	Left-to-right.
11	^	Bitwise XOR (Exclusive OR).	Left-to-right.
12	|	Bitwise OR (Inclusive OR).	Left-to-right.
13	&&	Logical AND.	Left-to-right.
14	||	Logical OR.	Left-to-right.
15	?:	Ternary conditional.	Right-to-left.
	=	Assignment.	
	+= -= *= /= %= <<= >>= &= |= ^=	Compound assignment.	
16	Throw	Throw exception.	Right-to-left.
17	,	Comma.	Left-to-right.

There are several subtle booby traps in here. For starters, operators with the same precedence level are evaluated from *left-to-right*, which means that the almighty rule of "perform division first" no longer holds. This can make a big difference depending on the data types and values involved. For example:

```
X80Percent = 80 * X / 100;
```

Here, the multiplication is performed *first*, so this seemingly innocuous expression could easily overflow, especially if working with 16-bit integers.

And, and here's an example where you want to test if some bit field is set. This is wrong:

```
if (ValueA | ValueB == 0xFF) {
    ...do something...
}
else {
    ...do something else...
}
```

You might expect that Logical OR is stronger than an Equality test, but it is not. Therefore, most of the time the second block above will execute. The code above should therefore probably read "if ((ValueA | ValueB) == 0xFF)".

As another example, here is some code that mixes floating point and integer arithmetic:

```
float f;
int i = 5;
int j = 2;
f = 1.0f + j / i;
```

In some languages you might expect the entire expression to be converted to floating point so that "f" is set to 3.5. However, in "C" the sub-expression "j / i" is evaluated first, and "5 / 2" in integer arithmetic discards the fraction, so this sub-expression has the value "2". This is then converted to floating point, to which we add "1.0", resulting in 3.0. The trick here is to understand how the compiler implicitly casts values.

Detection and Correction

A very common mistake is to enter "=" (assignment) where you intended to type "==" (equality test). Most compilers will issue a warning when you use "=" (assignment) in a conditional expression. Be sure to enable the maximum compiler warning level. Sometimes these are false warnings, but you can disable them with a #pragma or command line option *after you have verified and documented your intention*.

You can also use this common trick when comparing to a constant. Instead of typing:

```
if (x == 0)
```

type this "backwards" like this:

```
if (0 == x)
```

Since you cannot assign to a constant, you will get a compilation error if you accidentally type "=" instead of "==".

Other suggestions:

- Know your operator precedence.
- Simplify your expressions.
- It is pretty easy to mistype some of the logical operators &, &&, |, ||. Double-check your typing.
- Other cases are nearly impossible for the compiler or a Static Analysis tool to understand your intention, so

be sure to explicitly debug procedures that contain complex expressions.

- Order of evaluation can result in overflows and underflows. Use parentheses to group sub-expressions to avoid this.
- (When (in (doubt (use (copious (amounts (of parentheses)))))))).

Optimizer Errors

🐞 *Symptoms*: Application or system crash. Inexplicable behavior.

Although rare, compiler optimization errors (i.e., compiler bugs) do happen. Some that I have run into include:

- The compiler was generating a *signed* shift instead of an *unsigned* shift instruction. This resulted in the sign bit being replicated on a right shift, instead of filling in with zeroes. As a result, my character set conversion code was generating garbage. It took about two years before the compiler vendor finally fixed this, so I had to recode things on my side to make it work.
- My program was incorrectly sending data across a remote procedure call such that one of the parameters was sent twice, and one of the parameters was ignored. The problem went away after I disabled optimization for that routine.

Detection and Correction
This problem will typically manifest itself when the application works in a Debug build (where optimization is usually disabled), but fails miserably in a Release build.

After you have torn out most of your hair and decided "This is not me!" you don't have much choice but to study the generated machine code. If you find something suspicious you can disable optimization for that procedure with a #pragma, or for the file with a command line option. It is unlikely that the compiler vendor will immediately fix the problem so you can continue with your time-critical development, but reporting it will at least make you feel better.

Race Condition

Symptoms: Application or system crash. Inexplicable behavior.

A race condition occurs when processes or threads simultaneously operate on a shared resource in a conflicting way, thereby producing unexpected output. Consider this code:

```
if (NeedInitialization) {
        ...do some initialization work...
        NeedInitialization = FALSE;
}
```

Two threads can get beyond the "if" statement at the same time because thread scheduling either by the operating system or the processor is not predictable. If that happens, the inner code can be executed multiple times and will likely result in unexpected problems.

Detection and Correction

This is a difficult problem for either Static or Dynamic Analysis tools to detect, so you are pretty much on your own to code carefully. Some suggestions are:

- Be suspicious of any global variables that might be modified by multiple threads or processes, and add locks around access to those variables.
- Likewise, be suspicious of objects passed between threads through inter-thread messages and window messages.

To fix race conditions, use an appropriate lock when accessing the object (see the discussion under Deadlocks). The code sample above would then become:

```
LockObjects();
if (NeedInitialization) {
        ...do some initialization work...
        NeedInitialization = FALSE;
}
UnlockObjects();
```

Resource Leak

Symptoms: Application or system crash. Inexplicable behavior.

A "Resource Leak" typically refers to the failure to close a file. Eventually, the runtime system runs out of "file handles" (an opened file identifier), so it can no longer open any files.

Resource Leaks can also occur with database objects such as database and statement handles, TCP/IP socket connections, and similar subsystems that return a "handle" when some object is opened.

"Handles" are also used heavily in user interface code so the application can communicate with various windows and event objects.

Some trivia:

In the C runtime library for Visual C/C++ 2010, a process may open up to 2,048 files. In the days of MS-DOS, you could hack the C-Runtime and change "config.sys" to override the default limit of 20 files per process.

Unconfirmed, but apparently a Windows 2008 Server can open up to 16,384 files per session.

I don't know what the significance of this magic number is, but on my 64-bit Windows 7 system I could create 16,711,664 (0x7efff0) event handles before getting an error.

Unconfirmed, but apparently in Linux you can allow as many file handles as you want by tweaking various system configuration parameters.

Resource leaks can be hard to detect – you usually have to run the application for a significant amount of time before the problem occurs. For example, I had a resource leak that would only occur if you fed a broken input file to the application because the error recovery for the broken file case was incorrect. You would have had to hit this case about 1,000 times before a serious problem would occur, and it probably would have taken a few years of continuous operation before a resource leak would have become a problem, so I was lucky that nobody had run into this yet.

In a different application, I had a resource leak that resulted in loss of database connectivity at exactly the 101st activation. Rereading the database library documentation very carefully, I realized the problem, and fixed it quickly. Testing was not fun: I then had to make 101 telephone calls to confirm the fix.

Detection and Correction

A Static Analysis tool can usually find at least file handle leaks, and possibly leaks for other kinds of resources such as synchronization objects, database handles, and others. To find file handle leaks manually, search for all of the places that you open files, and make sure that the files are closed somewhere. In my experience, there is a simple and common pattern for file handle resource leaks happens with code like this:

```
fp = fopen(...);
if (fp == NULL)
    return error_code;
if (!do something to file) {
    return error_code;  // Missing fclose() call
}
...do something else...
fclose(fp);
return ok;
```

Other types of resource leaks may be a bit trickier to detect, so study your code carefully.

Resource Leaks and Memory Leaks can happen in C# and Java, too. For example, when you open a file, the runtime system eventually has to open the file via the operating system. The operating system returns a handle that is hidden inside the C# or Java file object, and is used internally when the application requests I/O services from the operating system.

If the object that encapsulates the file or other object is not destroyed properly (for example, if an exception occurs that bypasses closing the file), operating system-level resources will be leaked.

Most C# objects provide an "IDisposable" interface, which should be called in a *finally* block when you have finished using the object. The Dispose() routine is then responsible for cleaning up any operating system resources that it is using. Additionally, C# has a "using" statement which effectively calls Dispose() for you, even if an exception occurs.

Java Version 7 implements similar functionality using the *"try-with-resources"* syntax for objects that implement the AutoCloseable or Closeable interfaces.

Return Pointer to Stack Variable

Symptoms: Application or system crash. Inexplicable behavior.

It is perfectly "legal" to do this in C/C++:

```
int* p MyFunction()
{
    int i = 0;
    return &i;
}
```

This function returns the address of a *local* variable (a variable allocated on the stack). Upon returning from this function, the value of "i" is theoretically no longer defined, so you are playing with fire if you dereference the returned pointer.

The main reason somebody might want to do this is to do something *evil*. An exception to this might be with a debugging tool of some kind. Therefore, the majority of the time, returning a pointer to a local variable is either a mistake, or related to some evil intentions.

Detection and Correction

Most compilers will generate a warning when this is detected. Be sure to enable the maximum compiler warning level.

Otherwise, these are rather difficult to spot by eye, so a good Static Analysis tool can help to find these.

Security Breach

 Symptoms: Application or system crash. Loss of data.

I would actually consider a security breach to be the symptom of a bug, rather than a bug class by itself, but I have thrown it in here for discussion.

A malicious user can take advantage of application bugs to cause a "Denial of Service" attack. Such an attack can overload the system so that it becomes unusable by other users, or even cause a system crash.

Such attacks can be mounted either with knowledge of the source code or by trial-and-error using commonly known flaws such as inducing an overflow or SQL Injection. If the attacker has a copy of the executable program, it is not very difficult to disassemble it to find vulnerable entry points. Even without source code, C# and Java can be decompiled into quite readable source code, making it even easier for a would-be attacker.

Finally, client-server applications including Web applications need to be careful about privacy. Specifically, passwords and other sensitive information should be erased from memory once the information is no longer needed, and such information should only be transmitted using secure protocols.

Detection and Correction

You cannot entirely prevent a Denial of Service attack, but you can mitigate some of the effects:

- A good firewall will keep out malformed packets, which will first of all reduce some of the traffic inside the system, and also hopefully avoid downstream bugs that might be induced those packets.

- Keep your crowned jewels a secret! The less the outside world knows about your application, the more difficult it is to hack.
- As discussed elsewhere in this chapter, fix you bugs! Careless code can be an annoyance for most users, but an invitation to a hacker.

The following web sites have a great deal of information about bugs and security issues:

- http://www.cert.org
- http://cve.mitre.org

SQL Injection

Symptoms: Application or system crash. Security breach. Loss of data.

This became a hot topic especially when e-commerce became big in the late 1990s with the explosion of Internet availability. During the last ten years, we all wised up a lot, so you do not hear as much about this topic as you once did. However, newcomers to database programming need to be aware of what evil hackers try to do on purpose, and what silly end users can do by accident.

The two rules that you must always follow when accessing a database on behalf of the user are:

- Verify user input.
- Always use parameters.

Here's a nice little dynamic sSQL query:

"SELECT * FROM CustInfo WHERE CustID=" + *UserInput*

Everything will work very nicely until some wise guy inputs as the search data:

1234;DELETE FROM CustInfo

The problem here is the use of a dynamically generated query where the user input not only sets the data, but also the statements executed. Here, the user could enter ";", thus introducing another statement that can either expose additional data, or to do something destructive as I have done in this example. (In case you don't know SQL, I deleted *all* of the customer data!)

Detection and Correction

Some Static Analysis tools can detect potential SQL Injection problems. Or, you can also search for your DELETE, INSERT, SELECT, and UPDATE SQL statements without much difficulty to find potential SQL Injection spots.

The solution for avoiding SQL Injection attacks is simple: recode your queries to use SQL parameters so the queries. An ODBC query would look something like this:

"SELECT * FROM PopTunes WHERE Artist=?"

Then, you pass the value of *"UserInput"* as a parameter. In ODBC-compliant databases, "?" is a sequential parameter marker. In Microsoft SQL Server, parameters are of the form *"@parameter_name"*, and in Oracle they are of the form *":parameter_name"*.

When done this way, the database server will expand the query into a single statement with the parameter values filled in, and not expand this into multiple statements even if the data contains a special character.

Stack Overflow

 Symptoms: Application or system crash.

When an application uses too much stack space, hopefully it will fail quickly during the debug phase with a hardware-detected Stack Overflow error. In a worse case on simple hardware, the application can potentially overwrite non-Stack memory, potentially causing other kinds of failures.

Detection and Correction

I am not familiar with any tools that will help you determine the required stack size, although I am sure one exists somewhere. Most of the time you will probably only find out that you have a problem the hard way—after a stack overflow crash.

> The GNU compilers have a –fstack-usage option, which will create a file named *source_file*.su. This file lists the local storage required for each function in a compilation unit. This will give you some idea of the space required for local (stack) variables. However, you then need to manually figure out the worst case calling sequence, and you also need to add in the space required for passing parameters and the return address.

In my experience, you need stack space for no more than 20 to 25 calls deep in most applications (except when recursion is used). That means you need 4 to 8 bytes (for 32-bit vs. 64-bit systems) for each call, plus 4 to 8 bytes for each parameter. On top of this you will need space for each local variable.

To correct Stack Overflow problems, you need to determine which of these cases applies:

- A recursive procedure (a procedure that calls itself) eats all of the stack space. Make the stack larger, or change the algorithm, for example, to use *tail recursion*, where you do not really make a recursive call, but instead use a loop.
- Too many large objects allocated on the stack. Try allocating some of large objects in dynamic memory instead of using stack-based local variables.
- Increase the stack size.

The *reserved* (and maximum) stack size in a Windows desktop application a whopping 1 megabytes, and is specified on a per-executable basis. This is tremendous overkill in most cases, and a waste of virtual memory if you do not need it. Visual C++ users should check out the /Gs compiler option to control stack probe handling.

The maximum stack size on my Ubuntu desktop Linux system according to the "ulimit –s" command is 8192 (8MB). You can override this with the command "ulimit –s <stack_size_in_bytes>". You can also set the limit at runtime by calling the setrlimit() system function. GNU users should check out the -fstack-check compiler option for information on how stack checking is done.

The stack size for a new thread is specified when the thread is created. I typically set the thread stack size to 64KB instead of using the process default value. I also like to make the thread stack size configurable at the application level in case I find later that my 64KB guess was insufficient for some special case.

Undefined Behavior

 Symptoms: Undefined behavior.

No, the section title and the symptoms are not a typo.

There are places in the "C" and C++ specifications where particular statement forms produce *unspecified, undefined*, or *implementation-defined* behavior. In other words, the code may behave differently depending on the compiler used or the architecture that the application is executed on. In case you have not noticed, elsewhere in this book I use the expression "Inexplicable behavior" to make a distinction.

Even if you do not intend to run your application on multiple platforms, writing oddball code may fail the next time you upgrade your compiler, so you should avoid writing such code in the first place.

The main reason that these standards specify "undefined behavior", etc., is to allow for optimizations. For example, the expression "INT_MAX + 1" is "undefined" in the standard. If the compiler is evaluating a statement such as "if (xyz + 1 > xyz)", a lot of extra code is required to handle the actual common case where INT_MAX + 1 wraps back to "INT_MIN". However, if the compiler can ignore this case it can assume that "xyz + 1 > xyz" is always true, and thus avoid generating extra code that would degrade performance.

Some of the undefined behavior descriptions in the standard are largely unintelligible English—you must totally absorb the 500+ pages of the standard in order to understand the bizarre circumstances that they are discussing. And, a few of the cases seem like the committees were in too much of a hurry to finish up. For example, there is no standard behavior for certain cases of mismatched quotes and no standard behavior when you pass an invalid character to a character classification routine. It seems like they could have spent an extra five minutes deciding that "String constants must be terminated in the file in which the definition starts." They didn't, so lots of programmers waste hours tracking down mismatched quotes in include files.

The "C" language standard[5] contains 24 pages of scary exceptional behavior in Annex J. Every developer should review such specifications from time to time—you would be surprised at how many little things you do every day are actually potentially dangerous. The following table lists what I think are some of the more interesting ones. Descriptions and section references have been borrowed directly from the specification. My comments are in square brackets.

Section J1 – Unspecified Behavior

The value of padding bytes when storing values in structures or unions (6.2.6.1).

The value of a union member other than the last one stored into (6.2.6.1). [You probably knew this, but what happens elsewhere in the program if you access a union member that does not have the type that you expect?]

The values of any padding bits in integer representations (6.2.6.2).

The order in which sub-expressions are evaluated and the order in which side effects take place, except as specified for the function-call (), &&, ||, ?:, and comma operators (6.5). [Evaluation is usually left-to-right, but this is not guaranteed.]

The order in which the function designator, arguments, and sub-expressions within the arguments are evaluated in a function call (6.5.2.2).

The order of side effects among compound literal initialization list expressions (6.5.2.5).

The alignment of the addressable storage unit allocated to hold a bit-field (6.7.2.1).

Whether or not a size expression is evaluated when it is part of the operand of a sizeof operator and changing the value of the size expression would not affect the result of the operator (6.7.5.2). [This one is an English comprehension test. I gave up.]

The order in which any side effects occur among the initialization list expressions in an initializer (6.7.8).

The amount of storage allocated by a successful call to the calloc, malloc, or realloc function when 0 bytes was requested (7.20.3). [Anyone out there allocating *zero* bytes?]

The order and contiguity of storage allocated by successive calls to the calloc, malloc, and realloc functions (7.20.3). [Of course, but I suppose a beginner might make bad assumptions about the behavior here.]

The encoding of the calendar time returned by the time function (7.23.2.4). [The value is not necessarily the Unix-style time according to the language specification.]

The layout of storage for function parameters (6.9.1). [In other words, be careful if you are doing bit-fiddling of parameters.]

Which of two elements that compare as equal is matched by the bsearch function (7.20.5.1). [You can get into trouble if you have *similar* items in the data. Interested readers should study the topic *"stable sorting"* versus *"unstable sorting"*.]

The order of two elements that compare as equal in an array sorted by the qsort function (7.20.5.2). [Same as above.]

The value of the file position indicator after a successful call to the ungetc() function for a text stream, or the ungetwc function for any stream, until all pushed-back characters are read or discarded (7.19.7.11, 7.24.3.10).

Various places in this section: What happens when there are conversion errors in various math functions.

Finally, here is my own entry. The standard does not say what happens if the size of a table to be searched with bsearch() or sorted with qsort() is zero. Can the table pointer be NULL? Hopefully, the routine will do nothing, but this Unspecified Behavior is unspecified. (Got that? I mention this because I know of some analysis tools that will complain about this case.)

Section J2 – Undefined Behavior

An object is referred to outside of its lifetime (6.2.4). [These fall under my "inexplicable behavior" category.]

The value of a pointer to an object whose lifetime has ended is used (6.2.4). [This is a strange statement because the value is irrelevant. What is important is that you do not dereference it.]

The value of an object with automatic storage duration is used while it is indeterminate (6.2.4, 6.7.8, 6.8). [This causes my "inexplicable behavior" cases.

Conversion to or from an integer type produces a value outside the range that can be represented (6.3.1.4).

Demotion of one real floating type to another produces a value outside the range that can be represented (6.3.1.5).

An attempt is made to use the value of a void expression, or an implicit or explicit conversion (except to void) is applied to a void expression (6.3.2.2).

Conversion of a pointer to an integer type produces a value outside the range that can be represented (6.3.2.3). Conversion between two pointer types produces a result that is incorrectly aligned (6.3.2.3).

Two identifiers differ only in nonsignificant characters (6.4.2.1). [What are your compiler limitations? How long are your variable names?]

The program attempts to modify a string literal (6.4.5). [Are you modifying format strings on-the-fly?]

The characters ', \, ", //, or /* occur in the sequence between the < and > delimiters, or the characters ', \, //, or /* occur in the sequence between the "delimiters, in a header name preprocessing token (6.4.7). [This one is interesting! Lots of people code Windows-style paths in their include statements. For portability and this clause, the forward slash should be used.]

Between two sequence points, an object is modified more than once, or is modified and the prior value is read other than to determine the value to be stored (6.5). [Example: "i = ++i + 1;" and x[i++] = i;" have undefined behavior.]

Addition or subtraction of a pointer into, or just beyond, an array object and an integer type produces a result that does not point into, or just beyond, the same array object (6.5.6). [One beyond is okay, but more is *not* okay.]

Pointers that do not point into, or just beyond, the same array object are subtracted (6.5.6). [Same as above.]

The value of an object is accessed by an array-subscript [], member-access . or ->, address &, or indirection * operator or a pointer cast in creating an address constant (6.6). [Another English comprehension test in the specification. It sounds like the source code would be unintelligible anyway.]

An expression is shifted by a negative number or by an amount greater than or equal to the width of the promoted expression (6.5.7). [Darn it, sometimes I just want to throw away some bits!]

Pointers that do not point to the same aggregate or union (nor just beyond the same array object) are compared using relational operators (6.5.8). [This raises an interesting question: Where does a Standard Template Library iterator's end() really point to?]

An attempt is made to modify an object defined with a const-qualified type through use of an lvalue with non-const-qualified type (6.7.3). [Guilty.]

An attempt is made to refer to an object defined with a volatile-qualified type through use of an lvalue with non-volatile-qualified type (6.7.3).

A declaration of an array parameter includes the keyword static within the [and] and the corresponding argument does not provide access to the first element of an array with at least the specified number of elements (6.7.5.3). [It pays to read the specifications from time to time. I didn't even know you could do this, but I also found out that you can't do it with Microsoft C/C++ anyway.]

The } that terminates a function is reached, and the value of the function call is used by the caller (6.9.1). [Strange statement in the specification. Hopefully the compiler generates a "missing return" error.]

The name of a predefined macro, or the identifier defined, is the subject of a #define or #undef preprocessing directive (6.10.8).

A file with the same name as one of the standard headers, not provided as part of the implementation, is placed in any of the standard places that are searched for included source files (7.1.2). [I used to have to do this in the old days to increase number of file handles I could use.]

The value of an argument to a character handling function is neither equal to the value of EOF nor representable as an unsigned char (7.4). [Many of these functions are implemented internally as a table lookup, so a bad parameter will be looking beyond the end of the table. There is a similar undefined behavior case for wide characters.]

A byte input/output function is applied to a wide-oriented stream, or a wide character input/output function is applied to a byte-oriented stream (7.19.2). [This is disturbing if you work with internationalized applications.]

The string pointed to by the mode argument in a call to the fopen function does not exactly match one of the specified character sequences (7.19.5.3). [fopen() is unfortunately operating system dependent. On Windows, for example, you need a special mode to be able to process Unicode files properly.]

The file position indicator for a stream is used after an error occurred during a call to the fread or fwrite function (7.19.8.1, 7.19.8.2). [This is disturbing: You cannot determine the file size based on how far you have read?]

The stream for the fflush function points to an input stream or to an update stream in which the most recent operation was input (7.19.5.2).

The value of a pointer to a FILE object is used after the associated file is closed (7.19.3). [This is a strange statement in the standard. Is there an implementation that does useful things to an already closed file?] An output operation on an update stream is followed by an input operation without an intervening call to the fflush function or a file positioning function, or an input operation on an update stream is followed by an output operation with an intervening call to a file positioning function (7.19.5.3).

There are insufficient arguments for the format in a call to one of the formatted input/output functions, or an argument does not have an appropriate type (7.19.6.1, 7.19.6.2, 7.24.2.1, 7.24.2.2). [This is Undefined Behavior? It either blows up or prints garbage. GNU is pretty good at picking these out at compile time.]

The result of a conversion by one of the formatted input functions cannot be represented in the corresponding object, or the receiving object does not have an appropriate type (7.19.6.2, 7.24.2.2).

The value of a pointer that refers to space deallocated by a call to the free or realloc function is used (7.20.3). ["Inexplicable behavior" can result, especially in a multi-threaded application.]

The pointer argument to the free or realloc function does not match a pointer earlier returned by calloc, malloc, or realloc, or the space has been deallocated by a call to free or realloc (7.20.3.2, 7.20.3.4). [Microsoft C/C++ will generate a "heap corruption" runtime error. GNU generates an unfriendly stack dump with no explanation.]

Signal values other than SIGFPE, SIGILL, and SIGSEGV that correspond to a computational exception (7.14.1.1).

Various places in this section: What happens when various math exceptions occur.

Section J3 — Implementation-defined behavior

The number of significant initial characters in an identifier (5.2.4.1, 6.4.2). [Read your manual.]

The number of bits in a byte (3.6). [Does anybody remember the PDP-10? It used 7-bit ASCII in 36-bit words, and also had instructions to handle bytes of any size!]

Which of signed char or unsigned char has the same range, representation, and behavior as "plain" char (6.2.5, 6.3.1.1). [This is a pain in the neck for internationalized, multi-platform applications, especially when the compiler maker changes their default setting.]

Any extended integer types that exist in the implementation (6.2.5). [For example, __int64.]

Whether signed integer types are represented using sign and magnitude, two's complement, or ones' complement, and whether the extraordinary value is a trap representation or an ordinary value (6.2.6.2).

The results of some bitwise operations on signed integers (6.5).

The result of converting a pointer to an integer or vice versa (6.3.2.3).

The size of the result of subtracting two pointers to elements of the same array (6.5.6).

Whether a bit-field can straddle a storage-unit boundary (6.7.2.1).

The order of allocation of bit-fields within a unit (6.7.2.1).

The alignment of non-bit-field members of structures (6.7.2.1). This should present no problem unless binary data written by one implementation is read by another.

The places that are searched for an included < > delimited header, and how the places are specified or the header is identified (6.10.2). [Read the compiler manual carefully.]

The null pointer constant to which the macro NULL expands (7.17). [I recall PR1ME Computer, where NULL was *not* 0.]

Whether the file position indicator of an append-mode stream is initially positioned at the beginning or end of the file (7.19.3). [This is disturbing!]

Various places in this section discuss the current locale, and defaults for character conversion.

Enough! But, I hope you spotted a few that are bothersome to you. (I did.)

Unhandled Exception (Software)

 Symptoms: Application or system crash.

An "exception" is a way for a procedure to signal that it could not execute normally. For example, a routine that is supposed to read a file cannot execute properly if the file does not exist, so this routine might *throw* an exception. The calling procedure, in a *try* block tries to process the file by calling the processing routine, and if the processing routine fails, it can *catch* the failure exception.

In the old days, the failing procedure would simply return an error code. Somewhere along the road, some people thought that it would be more elegant to use the try/throw/catch model. There are arguments for and against each style. In my opinion:

- Nicely propagating an error return code up to the top level procedure can sometimes be as nasty as the main code itself. However, there is low overhead.
- There is significant overhead in setting up exceptions handling. For heavily exercised code, this is a waste of time unless exceptions are frequent.
- C++ users have to read more documentation to find out what exceptions might be thrown. It is much simpler knowing that a return value of "0" means "Ok", and non-zero means error.

I suppose that C++ exceptions do result in a cleaner application, provided they are not used excessively. The problem then, either with your own code or third-party code is remembering to *catch* all the possible exceptions that occur.

114

If you fail to catch an exception, it will bubble up to the top of the program, the runtime will find that there is no handler, and the program will be aborted with an "unhandled exception" error.

To make sure that you do not miss any C++ exceptions, it is a good idea to add a try/catch block near the very top of the program, something like this:

```
int main(int argc, char*argv[])
{
    try {
        ...main logic...
    }
    catch(std::exception& Ex) {
        ...handle outer exception...
    }
}
```

This is not a perfect solution, but it will give you a chance to collect some diagnostic information and to shutdown gracefully.

Finally, exceptions are the primary error handling mechanism in both C# and Java. The Java compiler has a nice feature that reports what exceptions you have forgotten to handle. For other languages you need to read the documentation!

Unhandled Exception (Hardware)

 Symptoms: Application or system crash.

Previously, I talked about software-generated exceptions. Additionally, all but the simplest processors have hardware-generated exceptions. The types of exceptions that can occur will vary by processor type.

For example, on an Intel x86, possible Protected-mode exceptions are: divide error, single-step/debug, nonmaskable interrupt, breakpoint, overflow, bounds check, invalid opcode, coprocessor available, double fault, coprocessor segment overrun, invalid TSS, segment not present, stack exception, general protection violation, page fault, and coprocessor error.

Other processors have similar kinds of hardware exceptions (although usually not quite as many).

The majority of the exceptions listed above are fatal and are handled by the operating system. However, you may want to handle some of these in user-mode applications.

Handling hardware exceptions is operating system specific. On Windows you need to use "Structured Exception Handling", and Unix-like systems you need to use "signals". Examples are given in "Chapter 10: Debugging Tips".

Floating Point Exceptions
Enabling Floating Point Exceptions (FPEs) allows you to detect divide by zero, overflow, and underflow errors.

Note that there is some funkiness involved here on an x86 — an overflow or underflow exception is not generated until the *next* floating point instruction is executed. Therefore, "x * y" might overflow, but the exception will not occur until you do another floating point operation. Therefore, if the full code is "z = x * y", an exception will be triggered because "store" is also a floating point operation.

On Linux you can use some C99 functions as in the following example:

```
#define _GNU_SOURCE
#include <fenv.h>

int main(void)
{
    double x, y, z;

    feenableexcept(FE_DIVBYZERO | FE_INVALID | FE_OVERFLOW);

    x = 1.0e300;
    y = 1.0e300;
    z = x * y; /* Causes an overflow FPE */

    return 0;
}
```

For Microsoft Visual C/C++, you can do two things:

- Use the _controlfp() or _control87() functions to control precision, and to enable or disable individual exception conditions.
- Use _clearfp() or _clear87() functions to clear pending exceptions.
- Use the /fp:except compiler switch. The compiler will generate different code if it knows that you will be handling exceptions yourself.

General Protection Violation

The x86 general protection violation exception covers a number of cases that normally will not happen in a stable user-mode application. However, in a long-running application, it is useful to catch "Access Violation" on Windows, aka "Segmentation Fault" on Linux.

These exceptions are caused by using an invalid pointer (for example, a NULL pointer), and are a symptom of a bug that needs to be fixed.

If you do not handle the exception, the operating system will display a scary error message, abort the application, and you will have an unhappy user. However, suppose this happens on a client-server system. If you do not handle this you may have not only a few hundred unhappy users, but a boss screaming at you about losing billions of dollars per microsecond.

I am always confident with my own code, but once in a while, you can hit a corner case in a library or driver that nobody ever thought of or is impossible to test before shipping. If you catch the exception—and you are lucky—the exception might be transient. Then, you might be able to keep the system alive until the evening when you can investigate in detail. (Also, by catching the exception you can capture a stack trace to assist in troubleshooting.)

Uninitialized Value or Pointer

🐛 *Symptoms*: Application or system crash. Inexplicable behavior.

In C/C++, most variables will be *uninitialized* by default. In other words, they will contain garbage that was either leftover when the machine was reset, or whatever value was leftover when some other code used the same memory. The exceptions are:

- *Global* variables. These are long-lived variables visible to the entire program, and will be initialized to zero by default.
- *Static* variables. These are long-lived variables visible either within a single file or procedure. These are also initialized to zero by default.
- Memory dynamically allocated with the calloc() runtime function.

Other variables are not initialized in consideration of performance. For example, it is certainly a waste of time to zero-out a 4KB buffer if the procedure is immediately going to fill the buffer from a file.

In contrast, all primitive data types in C# and Java are *theoretically* initialized to zero, and advanced data types are initialized to "null". However, both compilers actually complain if you try to use a variable that was not explicitly initialized, so it is not clear what the language designers were thinking. If you are zeroing local variables, it is therefore probably redundant, but you must do this to avoid the wrath of the compiler.

Regardless of the language, strange things can happen when an uninitialized variable is used, resulting in the various kinds of problems described elsewhere in this chapter.

Detection and Correction

Finding these cases is usually easy:

- Modern compilers will find most of these for you. Simply enable the maximum warning level to enable these messages.

  These same compilers are sometimes a bit obnoxious and falsely report uninitialized variable usage when you can see right in front of you that something will be set a few lines away. A common case is variables first set in a "try" block; the compilers that I know aren't quite smart enough to know that you *will definitely* go through this code in a moment. To get rid of the warning, just bite the bullet, initialize the variable, and leave a nasty comment to the compiler maker to make yourself feel better.

- Most Static Analysis tools can also detect uninitialized variables.

If the compiler or tool is unable to detect these, you may be in for some hard debugging to find, for example, your loop is running a random number of times, or why sometimes a routine almost works, but sometimes blows sky-high.

Use Pointer to Expired Object

 Symptoms: Application or system crash.

I have shot myself in the foot a number of times trying to do something like this in C++:

```
const char* pName;
   ...
if (!some_condition)
    pName = "Unknown";
else
    pName = GetNameAsStringObject().c_str();
   ...
printf("Name=%s¥n", pName);
```

All I am trying to do here is get a pointer to a string, and to avoid having to create a std::string object of my own. (So, why not cheat and get the std::string object only if necessary, but grab its internal pointer to the real string.)

Basically, don't use cheats like this. If you are using C++, stick with C++. Here, "GetNameAsString()" returns a std::string object, but you have no idea when the compiler will delete the returned value that it has stored in an automatically generated, hidden variable. In a lucky case, the value extracted via "c_str()" remains valid for a while, but you cannot depend on that, so this chunk of code sometimes works, and sometimes doesn't.

A correct implement would be more along these lines:

```
std::string Name;
        …
if (!some_condition)
   Name = "Unknown";
else
   Name = GetNameAsStringObject();
   …
printf("Name=%s¥n", Name.c_str());
```

Unfortunately, you have to swallow the overhead of always creating the string object, but you should make things work before you worry about making the world's most optimized code.

Detection and Correction

There is no easy way to detect these by inspection. Some Static and Dynamic Analysis tools can help to identify them.

Use After Free

Symptoms: Application or system crash. Inexplicable behavior. Data loss.

"Use After Free" means using a pointer after you have freed or deleted it, and this error is actually a variation of a "Dangling Pointer Dereference."

The coding pattern might look like this:

```
pData = (MyStructure*)malloc(sizeof MyStructure);
...do something to pData...
free(pData);
...do something else to pData...
```

Detection and Correction

While coding, do not use a pointer after you have freed it (or in C++, deleted it.) Other advice for this problem is exactly the same as for Dangling Pointer Dereferences.

There is no easy way to detect these by inspection. Static and Dynamic Analysis tools can help to identify them.

Weak Cryptography Problems

Symptoms: Application or system crash. Inexplicable behavior. Data loss, particularly private data.

Cryptography-related bugs can lead to unexpected system behavior including "denial-of-service" (down time of some sort), and possible exposure of private data.

Cryptography problems can be related to any of the bugs described in this chapter. Additionally, problems can be caused by any of the following:

- Use of an existing algorithm that is known to be flawed such as MD4, MD5, and SH1.
- Use of short security keys. The recommended length is *at least* 128 bits.
- The incorrect assumption that computer-generated random numbers are actually random.
- Weak, human-generated passwords.
- Incorrect design of a new cryptography method, or use of a new cryptography method that has not been proven by peer experts in the community.
- Weak storage of secret information. This includes, for example, storing account information as plain text, and leaving account information in temporary files.

Detection and Correction

Detecting cryptography problems involves a combination of detecting other kinds of bugs mentioned in this chapter either by manual methods or by using Static or Dynamic Analysis tools.

A lot of this also involves awareness and education, so if you have an application with critical security requirements, it is a good idea to assign someone to study the subject and to specialize in looking for such flaws.

WTH-CNI

 Symptoms: Hair loss. Insomnia. Substance abuse.

WTH-CNI stands for *"What The Heck – Completely No Idea!"*

This is the kind of bug where you write something, and you lose an entire week struggling with a ten line program that fails while trying to use a library for which you do not have the source code.

For example, recently I wanted to try a new feature in a library that I use. I copied, nearly verbatim, some code from the vendor's sample program, and the sample program does work. I've reread the documentation many times, and triple-checked all of my settings. No dice—I get an "invalid parameter" error. This error code is totally unhelpful because there are *dozens* of parameters in some complex data structures.

Usually when something like this happens, no one is able to help, and everybody keeps asking "How long will this take to fix?", adding to your misery.

People often ask me "How long does it take to write code versus debug it?". The answer is, "a ratio somewhere between 1:0.1 to 1:1000000." Ok, perhaps that's extreme, but this situation is not uncommon, so don't forget to add some slack time in your development time estimates.

Chapter Summary

The cost of fixing bugs can increase dramatically the further along you are in the development cycle. If the bug is detected by your "test team", you have wasted the test team's time! Testers should be validating software, not verifying it. If the

bug is detected in a released product, you will have angry—
and hopefully not injured—customers who use the time of
the support staff, who then have to go back to the testers to
reproduce the problem, who in turn go back to a maintenance
programmer or the original developer (if that person is still
around).

There are certainly other kinds of specific bugs. However,
those listed in this chapter are by far the most difficult to deal
with. Dealing with them early will avoid headaches, expense,
and damaged reputation problems down the road.

Chapter 4: Software Development Methodology

Despite incredible advances in computer hardware, software development remains somewhat of an art, and it lacks some of the discipline in other engineering fields.

This chapter discusses some of the more formalized development methodologies. You will learn about the traditional Waterfall Model. You will learn about the V-Model development method, which is used, for example, in embedded automotive applications designed around AUTOSAR and ISO 26262. Finally, you will also learn about various general-purpose Agile Software Methods such Crystal Methods, Dynamic Systems Development Model ("DSDM"), Extreme Programming ("XP"), Feature Driven Development ("FDD"), Scrum, and others.

Waterfall (Traditional) Model

The traditional approach to building something uses the "Waterfall Model"[6], a concept that comes from manufacturing and construction development techniques. When building something large such as an airplane or a ship, it is prohibitively expensive to start redesigning in the middle of the project. Therefore, each step or level in the "waterfall" is fully completed before committing to the next step.

Figure 1 - Waterfall Model

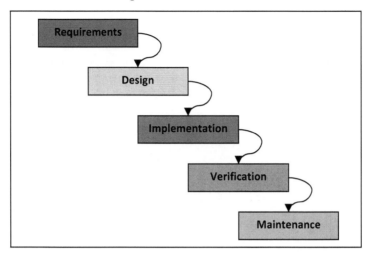

A design might look nice on paper, but it is of no use if manufacturing can't produce it. Therefore, Waterfall Model projects are usually a multi-disciplinary development effort involving everyone from designers through manufacturing people, and by the end of the design step everybody knows what to do to complete the process.

An advantage of the Waterfall Model is that it encourages up-front documentation.

A disadvantage of this approach in regards to software is that it does not leave much flexibility in adjusting the design late in the development cycle.

Some variations on the Waterfall Model include:

- Joint Application Development. Adds more customer involvement via JAD Workshops.
- Spiral. Adds prototyping and prototype refinement before the final product is built.

- PRojects IN Controlled Environments Version 2 (PRINCE2). A structured approach to project management endorsed by the U.K. government for public projects. Emphasizes breaking projects into small manageable phases, and provides guidelines for coordinating resources and managing difficulties.

V-Model

The "V-Model" is a variation of the Waterfall Model.

Figure 2 - V-Model

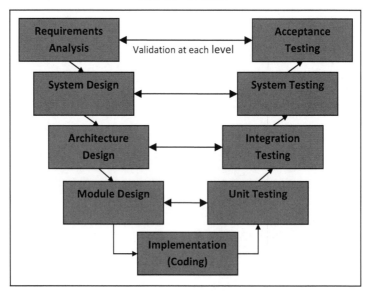

The V-Model places heavy emphasis on up-front design. It differs slightly from the Waterfall Model in that verification tasks (on the left side of the "V") are performed in parallel with validation tasks (on the right side of the "V").

The V-Model happens to be the development model recommended by ISO 26262 for safety-critical automotive applications, and these applications fall under the "Strict Development Environment" mentioned earlier. To develop such applications under this model requires detailed specifications, a huge amount of documentation, and a huge number of unit test programs. Therefore, such applications are typically designed using Unified Modeling Language (UML) tools and automated unit test generation tools.

General criticisms of the V-Model include:

- The up-front design approach is for project managers and bean counters, not for developers.
- There is limited ability for change.
- Testing is performed too late.
- Tests need to be designed in advance before any experimentation has been done.

You can find numerous rants on the Internet about why the V-Model is dead as a general development methodology.

Agile Software Development (ASD)

"Agile Software Development" refers to a group of *iterative* and *incremental* development techniques. Some of the more common ones are described in the following pages, followed by a discussion of the common themes and common terminology.

Crystal Methods[7]

Crystal Methods is a *family* of methodologies that focus on improving the interaction of people in lightweight development cycles. Key principles are:

- Frequent Delivery. Frequent releases (one to twelve weeks) allow the customer to spot problems quickly.
- Reflective Improvement. Frequent workshops are held so that everyone can contribute ideas for process improvement.
- Close Communication. Teams of six to eight people should work in the same room to promote fast and natural communication.
- Personal Safety. Team members must trust each other so that each member feels comfortable voicing an opinion.
- Focus. Developers must be able to understand and to concentrate on clearly defined goals, and to be able to perform tasks with a minimized level of interruption.
- Access to Experts. Developers need easy access to someone who is an expert in the business problem domain.
- Supporting Technical Environment. Requires automated testing, configuration management, and frequent integration.

It is worthwhile for managers to read up about Crystal Methods for ideas on managing projects with different levels of staffing and varying safety criticality.

Dynamic Systems Development Method (DSDM) [8]

A well-documented set of methodologies that focuses on human rather than technology issues based on the experience of DSDM Consortium members.

The current version of DSDM, "Atern", is first of all based on fixing the variables *time*, *quality*, and *cost*. This leaves *scope* (or *features*) as the remaining variable. The features implemented are based on a prioritized "MoSCoW" list: Must have, Should have (important, but not vital), Could have (would be nice if it won't break the budget), and W̲on't have (enough time in this budget).

Development proceeds based on the following eight principles:

- Focus on business needs.
- Deliver on time. Focus on the business needs priorities and "timebox" the development into short cycles.
- Collaboration. Create a single-team culture that includes some of the stakeholders. Ensure that members are empowered to make decisions with minimal bureaucracy.
- Never compromise quality.
- Build incrementally.
- Develop iteratively.
- Communicate continuously and clearly.
- Demonstrate control. Use formal and visible progress measurement. Continually measure viability with respect to business requirements.

The overall steps in a project are:

- Pre-Project. Describe a business need, identify a potential sponsor, and identify if the idea fits the business strategy of the organization.
- Feasibility. Establish if there are feasible solutions, benefits of the solution, and possible implementations.
- Foundations. Make the business case for the solution, define technical standards to be used, define how quality will be assured, establish project governance, describe basic schedule, and describe risk.

- Exploration. Expand on the Foundations step, produce a functional prototype.
- Engineering. Actual incremental and iterative development.
- Deployment. Install incremental or final product at customer site, train users, etc.
- Post-project. Assess whether goals have been achieved.

Atern defines a number of roles for people in the project:

- Business Sponsor.
- Business Visionary.
- Project Manager.
- Technical Coordinator.
- Team Leader.
- Business Ambassador.
- Business Analyst.
- Solution Developer.
- Solution Tester.
- Business Advisor.
- Workshop Facilitator.
- Atern Coach.
- Specialist.

A number of white papers and books are available at the DSDM online store[9] that describe these concepts.

A final note: DSDM is for internal use. You may not use it for external business without certification or a license.

Extreme Programming (XP) [10] [11]

XP aims to improve software development by creating an environment with these five key facets:

- *Constant communication* between team members and the customer.
- *Simple* software design.
- *Immediate feedback* through unit tests that are built along with the actual code. Components are delivered as soon as possible, and customer suggestions implemented as quickly as possible.
- Recognition of small successes leads to development of *respect* for team members and their unique contributions.
- The above allow XP developers to respond *courage*ously to changing to changing requirements.

The actual steps in iteration are:

- Planning. *User stories* are the customer-supplied, non-technical description of needs, typically only a few sentences long. The scope of the work is estimated, and is typically one to three weeks. If a story is too short it can be combined with something else; if too long, the story is split into smaller stories. These stories are also used to create *acceptance tests*.

  User stories are written on cards, and an overall *release plan* is developed with the cards while playing the XP-prescribed "Planning Game". Here, managers, developers, and the customer agree on the schedule and priority of the various stories.

  Detailed *iteration plans* are made just before each new iteration begins. In this step, specific programming tasks are determined. The results of any iteration are a deliverable to the customer.

- Management. The team works in an open area to promote communication, and the team should also have space for daily standup meetings.

People work in pairs to promote cross-training, and different pairs are used for different iterations. This ensures that everyone knows something about different parts of the system.

Project Velocity (number of user stories completed successfully) is measured. This value can be used in subsequent iterations to improve estimation skills. It can also be used in determining a reasonable velocity for a particular team.

- Designing. Keep it simple, but make sure that everyone knows the target system so they will create code with understandable names. Use object-oriented technology where possible. Create expendable "spike solutions" (separate throw-away programs) to explore implementation options as required. Do not add functionality that is not required now. Refactor often (i.e., redesign interfaces), and don't worry about trying to preserve legacy code that may be bulky in the new application.

- Coding. The customer is always available to fill in details that did not emerge during planning. Coding is done in a uniform style, and unit tests are always written *first*. All production code is done by a pair of programmers. Only one pair of programmers performs integration tasks at a time, and integration is done frequently on a dedicated integration computer.

Collective Ownership of the code means anybody can add code, refactor, or fix bugs. Confusion in this area is prevented by requiring that all code submitted to a repository include unit tests that test 100% of actual code.

- Testing. All code must have unit tests, and unit tests must run 100% successfully before check-in to the repository. When a bug is fixed, a regression test is also added. Black box acceptance tests are created early in the planning stage, are run frequently, and the scores are published. This is referred to as "Test-Driven Design" (TDD).

Proponents of Extreme Programming say that it allows test-drive software to be designed for today (not for a few months from now), and developed without dependence on the in-house superstar programmer.

Critics of Extreme Programming say:

- Emphasis on "mini-design" at the iteration level results in wasted time. The design requirements will change frequently as new user stories are added.
- The customer representative is likely to be a junior person who is not the expert required for success. Furthermore, you have to negotiate with the customer at each iteration; over many iterations this is time-consuming and frustrating for everyone.
- The unit tests catch code-level bugs, but not design-level bugs.
- XP encourages frequent refactoring, but this only makes sense in XP where there is no master design in the first place. Otherwise, excessive refactoring can waste a large amount of time.
- Programming in pairs is difficult and not necessarily productive.
- Customers will not do business with you unless they also understand XP.
- XP methods imply limited documentation.

Feature Driven Development (FDD)[12]

FDD is a combination of Agile Methods and software modeling. The main concepts in FDD are:

- FDD development starts with building a broad object model. The purpose of the model is not to make a final design, but more to allow the team to understand the problem domain. The model is probably not the final model, just something to kick-start the process.
- The second step in FDD is to develop a required feature list based on the object model. Features of the form "<action> <result> <object>", each requiring one to five days are listed. Features that will take more than a week are decomposed into smaller features.
- Related features are organized into *activity* sets, and assigned to Chief Programmers. Unlike other ASD methods, there is no *collective ownership* concept. The reasoning behind this is that there should be one expert in a particular area, and that expert is the one who can make changes most quickly. (With collective ownership, everyone knows a little bit about everything.) Additionally, the expert can take pride in his or her specific part.
- The Chief Programmer assembles a small "feature team" for each activity. Iterations for one team do not need to be synchronized with other teams.
- Features are built, are unit tested, and code review is done. The code review helps to find bugs not exposed in testing, allows less experienced developers to learn faster, and forces everyone to code according to the standard being used.
- Progress is made highly visible, particularly through *"Parking Lot Charts"*.

- Regular builds are performed to expose integration problems, and to ensure that there is always a working version.
- Configuration Management is performed to maintain each and every artifact involved including source code, documents, test cases, test results, change logs, contracts, and other material.

FDD works with large teams, whereas most ASD methods work best with small teams.

Lean Software Development[13]

Lean Software Development is more of a thought process than a set of specific methodologies. This thought process is based on "lean manufacturing techniques" including ideas borrowed from Toyota Corporation's philosophy. The seven "Lean Principles" are:

- Eliminate Waste. This includes unnecessary functionality, unclear requirements, bureaucracy, slow or ineffective communications and processes, and defects.
- Amplify Learning. Increase feedback including early feedback from the customer. Shorten time to feedback by having frequent iterations. Run automated tests frequently.
- Design as Late as Possible. Product requirements change, so design is based on actual customer requirements, not guesswork.
- Deliver as Fast as Possible. Quick delivery through iterations allows customers to delay decisions too, and enables rapid customer feedback.
- Empower the Team. Allow the team to work effectively by enabling self-determination, self-motivation, leadership, and expertise through training, collaboration, and standards.

- Build in Integrity. Create simple, clear code with built-in unit tests and acceptance tests. No code repetition and no extra features.
- See the Whole. While the "Lean Principles" encourage fast delivery, remember to stand back, look at the whole process, and make sure you are also moving in the direction of the overall business goals, too.

Rapid Application Development (RAD)[14]

The essential elements of RAD are:

- Methodology. Timeboxed, iterative prototypes using Computer-Aided Software Engineering (CASE) tools and active customer involvement.
- People. Key players are the Sponsor, User Coordinator (liaison for the Sponsor), User Coordinator (project manager on the customer side), Requirements Planning Team (high-level users who decide the required features in planning workshops), User Design Team (Requirements Planning Team plus additional users who may have more detailed knowledge of the requirements), User Review Board (user-side testers), Training Manager, Project Manager, SWAT Team (two to six Skilled Workers with Advanced Tools, i.e., the developers), and Workshop Leader.
- Management. People committed to RAD who are able to motivate the players, able to use and demonstrate performance measurement tools, and able to cut through political obstacles.
- Tools. Extensive use of CASE, automatic code generation, code re-use, and diagramming tools to aid in design and to clarify thinking.

The primary criticism of RAD is that both developers and customers tend to place too much emphasis on the visual aspects of the application (the "GUI") and therefore might not pay enough attention to solving the underlying business problem.

Most variations of ASD use RAD development tools, at least for generating user interfaces.

Scrum[15] [16]

The term "Scrum" is borrowed from rugby, where the two teams "huddle" to initiate the next play. For software development, the two teams are the *customer* and the *developer*, and the process is as follows:

- A *product owner* is a representative of the *stakeholder* (the customer). This person creates a prioritized list of desired features called the *product backlog*.
- For each *sprint* cycle (typically two to four weeks), the team selects a digestible set of tasks from the backlog and decides how to implement the selected subset.
- Each sprint is followed by a *sprint review* where the team can reflect on the outcome.
- The sprints repeat until the backlog has been fully implemented, the deadline has been reached, or the budget has been exhausted.

Whatever the reason for ending the sprints, the process guarantees that at least the most desired features have been implemented.

The major criticisms of Scrum relate to giving too much control to the Product Owner, who oftentimes is not a software engineer. Frequent change requests from the Product Owner can result in distraction from the original goal, demoralization of team members who have a better feeling for the intricacies of getting to the goal, and difficulty estimating overall costs because the task may not be well defined.

Scrum is thus said to be better for small, short-term projects such as web development.

Related: Toyota Production System (TPS)[17]

Many concepts of Lean Software Development are based on concepts from TPS, with its easy-to-remember principle of *elimination* of _muda_ (waste), _mura_ (inconsistency), and _muri_ (overburden).

TPS is more about building automobiles, but the concepts are interesting, and the philosophy can be applied to software development.

Other Methodologies[18]

The reference list contains links to dozens of other variations of Agile Software Development.

Common Themes in ASD

Common to most of these methodologies are the following concepts:

- Iterative, incremental design and development.
- Timeboxing.
- Immediate testing.
- Self-organizing, adaptive teams.
- Focus on people, not the product.
- Small, co-located teams to facilitate immediate interaction.

- Customer-driven.
- The code is the documentation.

Here's my opinion on these.

Iterative, Incremental Design and Development

There are too many intangibles in an abstract software design. In Agile Software Development, the project is therefore broken down into very small chunks. Feedback from the results is used to decide the next steps, thus allowing the design to be modified as you go.

One thing to be careful about is to not go massively off course, as this may obviously result in breaking the original budget.

Timeboxing

In time management, the concept of a "time box" is to consider three variables: *time*, *quality*, and *scope*. Since quality is a natural requirement, timeboxing limits development goals to short cycles (e.g., one week or one month), which will then limit the scope of the development for that period.

This approach allows the roadblocks in technical or team-related issues to be identified early on.

This happens to be how I work all the time, except my timebox is almost always one *day* when I am working by myself. Each day I pick one or more items of high priority that can be accomplished by the end of the day, and do it. I hate leaving something half done, so some days turn out to be long days when the selected item was a bit too ambitious.

Immediate Testing

With short development cycles, software needs to be tested before it is ever checked-in to the master product repository. The rule is basically "never break the system". Therefore, unit-tests need to be developed in parallel with the main code.

I have some difficulty with this concept in a few scenarios:

- How do you develop automated tests for code that requires human interaction (e.g., mouse-driven user interface code?).
- Writing unit tests for event-driven code such as in a telecommunications or network application takes more time than writing the code itself. This makes sense if you are building critical systems, but in some projects may not be practical.
- Writing code that can be unit-tested may likely change the way that the code is designed, and that may not be the optimal design.
- Unit tests may not necessarily detect problems at the system level, so even more complex system-level tests are generally required.

Unit tests are a necessary evil in some applications. In some applications, though, creating so many unit tests early on as suggested by ASD can waste a lot of time if you are just experimenting or prototyping.

Self-organizing, Adaptive Teams

Small teams capable of organizing themselves, respecting each other, and working in a small area where people can communicate instantly is an important factor in getting the "incremental" work units done.

This requires a certain level of business sense in the team; if you don't have this you need to hire a better mix of people. Certainly, an occasional nudge in the right direction might be required, but good engineers *just know* what to do. If you have people who don't know what to do, get rid of them, and then don't micro-manage the rest of the people or you will cause hard feelings.

Focus on People
Management needs to focus not on the end result, but on facilitating the developers to get the job done. The developers are highly-motivated, talented people who know how to do their job, and management's job is to clear away any obstacles. Don't forget to reward them—a challenging project is not necessarily fun, and if there is no motivation, the people will leave for greener pastures.

Small, Co-located Teams
Working side-by-side promotes immediate communication. Even though e-mail is fast and Skype conferences are free, there's nothing like face-to-face contact when trying to work out a problem.

As for team structure, the teams need people with complementary skills. I like the concept of having a limited number of *chief programmers* who do final coding and integration, while other members develop prototype code and tests. And, this organization solves coding style problems since you limit the number of people feeding final code into the master product.

This is certainly an ideal case. If you cannot implement this organization perfectly, be sure that everyone has plenty of Internet and mobile phone access to each other.

Customer-Driven

All ASD techniques involve more direct contact between the developers and the customer than with more traditional techniques. Developers can get a much better idea of what to do if they understand how the customer operates. Likewise, customers can understand better what they have asked for when they can get direct and immediate feedback.

This is great, provided that the customer is providing *useful* feedback. I recall a project where we were a few days from the deadline, and the customer representative was wasting a key developer's time with a lot of time on non-critical requests such as "Can you make this button a little darker blue?". (It would have looked different in different light or a different display, anyway.) You *do* need to keep *some control* over the situation—remember that the timeboxed goal should have been established in the beginning of the cycle.

The Code Is The Documentation

Agile Modeling has a rant something like "Documentation affects the Total Cost of Ownership, and is usually out of synch with the development, so you have to ask yourself if you really want it."

This makes some sense for a simple, evolving system that is likely to be short-lived. It makes no sense for a complex system or a system that is likely to be used for five years or longer. The original developers are likely to move along to other projects or companies; figuring out how a complex system works by looking only at the code is *very* time-consuming.

ASD Methods Comparison

The ASD variations above all sound somewhat alike, so here is a summary of the differences.

Table 10 - ASD Methods Comparison

	Crystal	DSDM	FDD	Scrum	XP
Approach	Incremental.	Iterative.	Iterative.	Iterative increments.	Iterative increments.
Timebox	Depends on Crystal family.	80% of total time.	Two days to two weeks.	Two to four weeks.	One to six weeks
Team Size	Any.	Any size with independent teams.	Any size with multiple teams.	Any size with multiple Scrums.	< 20.
Project Size	Any.	Any.	Complex projects.	Any.	Small.
Communication	Informal, face-to-face.	Documentation.	Documentation.	Informal daily standup.	Informal daily standup.
Customer Involvement	Receives releases	Receives frequent releases.	Receives reports.	"Product Owner Role".	Customer is team member.
Documentation	Basic.	Documentation exists.	Documentation is important.	Basic.	Basic.
Specialties	Adaptable method family, any project and team size.	Prototyping.	UML Diagrams.	Sprints, Product and Sprint backlogs, Planning Poker, Scrum Master.	TDD, User Stories, Refactoring.
Pros	Methods adjust to project size and type.	Requirements priority, efficient project management.	Documentation and reports enable multitasking.	High level of communication and collaboration.	Open workspace, customer is part of team, well defined best practices, feedback.
Cons	Difficult to coordinate bigger teams.	Complex documentation.	Individual code ownership except with small projects.	Weak documentation, poor project control.	Weak documentation, customer must be present, lack of discipline.

Relationship to Bugs

The management and development style of a project is not going to eliminate bugs. However, the style will certainly influence people's behavior, and hopefully in turn will reduce the number of bugs. Here are some thoughts:

- Timeboxing and Unit Tests. If you use a Waterfall approach and find a horrible bug at the end, you may be in big trouble because the bug affects a large portion of the design. By developing in small increments, bugs will hopefully be exposed earlier.
- Focus on People. Keeping people happy and not overworking them is very important. If people are too tired or are not enjoying their work, the number

of errors is probably going to increase. When I work on something interesting, I will often work for 18 hours straight. However, there comes a point where I am so tired that it becomes dangerous using the computer. It is too easy to delete something important or to make a major editing mistake; this is the time to shut off the computer, and go relax or go to sleep.

- Small, Co-located Teams. Sometimes a developer just gets stuck on a simple piece of code. You can stare at it for hours, and cannot spot what is a wrong. If you can explain your problem to the person at the next desk, if that person cannot spot it, probably you will as you explain it. (When working at home, I often explain things to my wife. She could care less, but she pretends to listen, and I usually I figure out my problem.)
- Access to Experts. This is certainly helpful. With enough time you can usually figure out anything, but the expert can save you a lot of time.

Chapter Summary

There are a number of formal and semi-formal project management methodologies. Think about them. Discuss them. Adapt them for your team. All of them are designed to improve teamwork, reduce cost, reduce time-to-market, and to help everybody keep their wits.

Chapter 5: Bug Avoidance: Your Tools

This chapter discusses the tools you need to successfully implement a software project.

Management Methodology

Choose a management methodology at the outset of the project. Some options are discussed in the previous chapter, particularly under "Agile Software Development". Adopt one, or adapt a combination of them to suit your needs.

Make sure everyone knows the game plan.

Programming Language

The programming language you choose will be determined by (1) what the developers already know, (2) what the customer requires, (3) portability considerations, and (4) the application domain.

Here are some of the pros and cons of various languages.

Table 11 - Brief Comparison of Programming Languages

	C	C++	C#	Java
Portability	Excellent	Excellent	GUI code only on Windows	Excellent
Performance	Excellent	Very good	Good	Good
Internationalization	Difficult	Difficult	Simple	Simple
Ease of GUI development	Good	Good	Very Good	Very Good
Open Source UML Tools	Limited	Limited	Limited	Many

(I mention Open Source UML tools above because if you want to use UML, you have to study both UML concepts and the tool itself, so it's nice to have something free that you can play with. There also plenty of commercial UML tools for all of the languages mentioned above.)

I always choose C/C++ for heavy duty work. For simpler work, especially if there is a graphical user interface involved, I use either C# or Java. Java is more portable than C# because C# "windows forms" only run on Windows. So then I decide based on the target audience: Is this just for Windows users, or a multi-platform application? If it is Windows-only, I prefer C# simply because end-users will have fewer add-ons to install (the ".Net Framework" runtime will probably already be installed). For multiplatform, though, Java is a better choice, although many Windows users will end up having to install the Java Runtime Environment.

Regarding just language features, I personally happen to prefer C# over Java because:

- Setting up non-default values in Java enumerators is unpleasant.
- Iterator usage is ugly.
- To set up object properties you have to write "setter" and "getter" functions. In C# you can generate properties and handlers almost automatically.
- I don't like typing domain names, which are used in object names, backwards!

Operating System

As long as I am on the subject of programming languages, I might as well discuss operating systems.

If you are designing consumer-oriented applications, clearly you target one or more of a desktop edition of Linux, Mac OS, or Windows. For "server" applications, there are many choices including AIX, a BSD-derived systems (see below), HP-

UX, a server edition of Linux, Solaris, Windows Server, and others. Finally, for mobile applications you will likely target iOS and Android, and possibly a few others.

For BSD-derived systems, you have lots of choices, the main ones being FreeBSD, NetBSD, and OpenBSD. The BSD licensing is much more business-friendly than systems based on the GNU Public License ("GPL"), the code is of high quality and high performance, so the distinguishing point is in the licensing terms. The most common use I see of BSD-derivatives is in embedded systems, routers, and firewalls.

There are many other choices for embedded applications including iTron-based systems such as T-Engine and TOPPERS, LynxOS, OSE, QNX, RTLinux, VxWorks, and Windows CE.

Coding Standard

Pick a standard and make everybody stick to it.

Your choice of a standard may be dictated by what you are building, as discussed in "Chapter 6: Development Standard and Specifications".

Comments and Documentation

These days, following a coding standard also specifies the style of writing in-code comments. The stylized comments allow various tools to be used to automatically create internal documentation. Such tools include:

- Doxygen. Open Source document generator for C, C++, Java, and many other languages. This can create internal documentation in many output formats, and can graphically show the dependencies between modules.

- JavaDoc. The standard Java documentation generator.
- Microsoft SandCastle. Integrated with Visual Studio since Visual Studio 2005. Can create internal documentation and user-level help files.
- Other. There are many other tools, both Open Source and proprietary. [19]

The main trick in using these tools is to get people to write and maintain *useful* comments in the first place. Additionally, somebody will need to manually write some "roadmap" documentation because just spitting out a list of available functions does not help newcomers delve into a monstrous application.

Code Review

Code Review, where team members inspect each other's code, should be performed on a regular basis. The main reasons are:

- It provides an opportunity to confirm that everyone is focusing on the project requirements.
- It provides an opportunity to catch possibly strange implementations of a solution before too much effort has been applied. "Two (or more) heads are better than one", so peer review is a chance for the team members to suggest alternate ways of solving a complex problem.
- It is an opportunity to spot violations of agreed upon coding style rules. You should be careful, though, to prevent code review from turning into a coding style war where everyone goes away angry and feeling degraded.

Development Tools

Make sure you have the right tools, as discussed below.

Hardware

In the "old days" when I had a 10MB hard drive on my 8Hz CPU, I would literally go out for the afternoon whenever I needed to recompile my whole application.

Machines may still not be as fast as you'd like for multi-million line projects, but get the best machines you can afford for your developers. You can pay them to sit around waiting for the machine, or you can keep them busy by helping them get results faster.

If you buy notebooks, don't buy the cute little ones with a compact keyboard. They are ok if you need to use them on a crowded train, but are difficult to type on, and will lead to shoulder pains and carpal tunnel syndrome.

These days I use a laptop computer with 750GB hard disk, a quad-core 64-bit CPU, and 8GB of memory, and I am hoping soon to double the memory and add a second drive. This allows me to have lots of Virtual Machines, so I can run Windows 7 as the main "host" system, and Windows XP and several variations of Linux and BSD Unix all on one system.

Working with Virtual Machines is much less troublesome than trying to boot multiple operating systems. The performance penalty versus running the other operating systems is tiny, and the ability to be running multiple operating systems at once is absolutely wonderful. All you need to be careful about is to provide adequate memory.

Finally, there are many software-based emulators available today, so it is a breeze, for example, to debug code for an ARM-targeted system on your Intel or AMD-based PC.

Software

Do you have the right tools? You don't necessarily need the latest and greatest IDE and compilers, but are you using some outdated, unsupported, buggy thing? Or, are you using a tool that just came out last week, and still has some glitches?

IDE

There are *many* Integrated Development Environments (IDEs) available. An IDE runs the tools a developer needs to create an application: project creation and configuration, an editor, compiler, linker, debugger, screen designers, and other tools. Some that I have experience with are:

- CodeWarrior. A multi-platform, multi-target IDE originally developed by Metrowerks, and now owned by Freescale. CodeWarrior focuses on building embedded applications. A "Processor Wizard" can be used to automatically generate a lot of the required low-level code.
- DialogBlocks. A cross-platform tool for building the user interface portion of applications.
- Eclipse. A Java-based, Open Source IDE. It is primarily oriented towards Java development, but the "plug-in architecture" allows it to be used for other languages including C/C++.

  There are many customized versions of Eclipse for specific environments. For example, the Android SDK, Tizen SDK, and many products from IBM are based on

Eclipse. Eventually, you will probably run into Eclipse, so it is useful to learn this tool.

- Renesas HEW. This is primarily for embedded applications based on chips such as the "SH4". An automatic code generator can be used to create a lot of the low-level, processor-specific code.
- Microsoft Visual Studio. This is primarily for building applications for Windows running on Intel-style CPUs, but add-on packages also allow targeting other processors for mobile editions of Windows.

  The "Express" (free) edition of Visual Studio is suitable for basic development, but you cannot use any third-party plug-ins, and you cannot create an installer package from the IDE. (For installers you can use the Windows Installer XML ("WiX") toolkit if necessary.) If you want all of the bells-and-whistles in one package, you should look at the "professional" variations.
- Xcode. Apple's IDE for creating applications for Mac OS and iOS.

Learning a new IDE takes several days. People have to learn a new editor, learn where all of the project and compiler settings are hidden, and figure out how to import existing projects and source code, and how to use the debugger. Arrange a short, in-house class for everyone to save time.

Compilers
Use your compilers well:

- Enable the maximum warning level, and strive for *zero* warnings. If you get an annoying warning that is false, you can usually disable the particular warning with either a #pragma statement or a command line option. But, do take the time to confirm that the warning is *not* a problem.

- Avoid compiler-specific features as much as possible.

If you have time, I suggest that you try multiple compilers early in the development. This helps to keep the code clean because different compilers produce different warnings. The GNU "C" and C++ compilers are particularly loud-mouthed when it comes warnings, but they are very good at picking out things that are difficult for a human to spot. Examples of this include "extern" statements that are no longer necessary and are just cluttering the code, and format string/argument mismatches that may later lead to a runtime error.

Debuggers
Master your debugging tools:

- If it is a somewhat complicated debugger such as GNU's "gdb", print out the associated cheat sheet.
- Knowing the machine architecture and it's assembler language may be helpful when you hit really hairy bugs including compiler optimization errors.

Modeling Tools
This is a rather large topic just by itself, but you might want to look into Computer Assisted Software Engineering (CASE) and Unified Modeling Language (UML) tools for complex projects. Some tools can be used for to generate the overall structure and to assist in visualization of the requirements, and some tools can even generate large portions of the code.

Dynamic and Static Analysis Tools

There are a variety of tools to assist in bug detection. Some are free or Open Source, and some are commercial packages. Anything is better than nothing—use any tools available to you, and use them as early as possible in the development cycle. These are discussed later in "Chapter 8: Analysis Tools".

Extra Documentation

The Internet "revolution" more or less destroyed the publishing industry (to the benefit of the environment), but is also means that the developers need Internet access for simple research, finding basic documentation, and for finding help from other people having similar difficulties.

However, a few good books can come in handy too, and some books should be in your development budget. Depending on the application, you may also need to budget some official specifications from ISO, ITU, MISRA, and other places.

Incidentals

You may need some of the following depending on the nature of the project:

- In-Circuit-Emulators (ICEs). Used for debugging embedded applications.
- Prototype computers. Circuit boards that plug into an ICE so you can develop a smartphone or other embedded applications before the production devices are available.
- Wireshark (formerly Ethereal). A software datascope for debugging LAN applications. http://www.wireshark.org.

- Datascope. Useful for debugging communications applications.
- Oscilloscope. Sometimes useful when debugging device drivers.
- Real Devices. Production-quality smartphones, tablets, or other embedded devices.
- Printer Ink.
- A whiteboard for brainstorming.
- Lots of soft drinks. For me, lots of coffee!!

Work Environment

A suitable work environment is crucial. Generally speaking, small, co-located teams work best. Plenty of light, and plenty of quiet are a must. I have to admit that I am guilty of making too much noise. I am used to working in my own private space, and I tend to complain aloud to the computer a lot. In an open office, this soon becomes confusing and annoying.

Allow flex time—to a point. Expect easy days and hard days, but try to make sure everyone is working some core hours. It irked me to no end one time when I was involved in a large project where I was literally working the "banker's hours", but a lot of other key members were not showing up until the afternoon, and then would work through the evening. Besides making a bad impression on the customer, these people completely missed the opportunity to learn how the customer's business worked.

Minimize interruptions—people cannot very well concentrate on development when they are constantly interrupted by telephone calls, unscheduled meetings, unscheduled demonstrations, and, yes, annoying bosses. Assign some people to filter telephone calls. Avoid anything unscheduled.

Limit the number of active projects—Efficiency will decrease if a developer is working on too many projects at once. It takes a while to switch gears in your mind. If someone is working on a significant project, let them concentrate on it. If they have multiple projects to work on, try limiting how many gear switches there are per day—otherwise, most of the productive time will be lost. I typically have half a dozen projects going on, but I try to work on only one or two in a single day, reserving certain days for certain projects

Finally, minimize time pressure. Time pressure is sometimes be unavoidable, but constant time pressure will just drive people away.

Encourage Breaks
When I have a software problem, this works for me almost every time: Stop thinking about it.

Oftentimes, just getting out of the office and talking a walk around the block will do the trick. Other times, a good night's sleep, taking a nice hot bath in the winter, or taking a refreshing cool shower in the summer works. I always try to keep a pen and notebook handy in case I have a brainstorm while I am theoretically not thinking about something.

Encourage people to take a break when they get stuck.

Say Thank You
Programmers are people, too. Unfortunately, rarely does anyone say "Thank You" to them, either for fixing a problem or developing something cool. Showing some appreciation goes a long way.

It works the other way, too. Programmer's should thank the sales and marketing team. Your salary doesn't come out of thin air. (Exception? You may beat up sales people when they have sold something that doesn't exist, and caused you a lot of grief!)

Open Source

Many organizations are against anything "Not Invented Here." On the other hand, you can often save a lot of development time if you can leverage existing, Open Source code that has hopefully already been debugged. Then, the main thing to worry about if you are developing a commercial application are the license conditions, as discussed below.

Open Source Licenses

Commercial-friendly licenses include Apache, Berkeley Software Distribution (BSD and the 3-clause "New BSD"), Massachusetts Institute of Technology (MIT), and for some restricted cases the GNU Lesser General Public License (LPGL).

The main things that you need to be aware of when using Open Source code in a proprietary application are:

- Are you required to make your application available for free? (Beware of GPL and others.)
- Can you mix code using different licenses? What happens if you are mixing code covered by a mixture of licenses such as GPL, BSD, and Apache?
- Do you need to expose your proprietary code?
- If you modify (fix or enhance the code) an Open Source project are you obligated release your modifications to the public?

- Do you have or use patented code? (Beware of GPL and others.)
- Take the licenses for Is there a difference between statically linking and dynamically linking to a library? Statically linking to a library may make your application fall into the class of a *derivative application*, whereas dynamically linking may not. For the latter case, many libraries may fall under a less restrictive license such as LGPL instead of GPL.
- the code that you are using seriously. For example, the U.S. Federal Circuit court ruled in Jacobsen v. Katzer (535 F.3d 1373-2008) that not abiding by the terms and conditions of an Open Source license qualifies as a copyright infringement. As such, infringement is a federal offense subject to the infringing party paying damages, and with potential of an injunction.

I was recently looking into the definition of "derivative works", specifically in regards to "device drivers", and I found:

- The Free Software Foundation considers "plug-in" (e.g., for a browser) as a derivative work if it runs within the host application, and hence is against the GPL. On the other hand, if the so-called plug-in runs in a separate process, it is not considered a derivative work, and hence you are clear.
- If a software component is not essential to system operation, and hence can be shipped and installed separately, you might be clear.
- The issue of drivers is rather odd in respect to the above—who's process does the driver run in?

- Finally, if "a thread is lightweight process", is anything that runs in a multi-core processor or multi-threaded application exempt from GPL restrictions? (Sorry, I just had that perverted idea and couldn't resist throwing it in.)

You need to be careful when using Open Source in a proprietary application, especially when the GPL is involved. If in doubt, contact a lawyer, or contact the original developer regarding commercial licensing terms.

Documentation

One of my major complaints about a lot of Open Source software is that the documentation is generally sub-par. Therefore, when evaluating such a package be sure that you are not going to waste a huge amount of time just trying to figure out how it works.

Below are some of the Open Source packages that I think are useful and/or just cool.

Table 12 - Some Useful Open Source

Name	Description	License
antlr	Another Tool for Language Recognition (i.e., a parser generator). You will probably need to buy the author's book "The Definitive ANLTR 4 Reference" by Terry Parr to make effective use of this tool.	BSD
chromium	Open Source web browser, base of Google Chrome.	Google-authored portions use BSD license; other licenses apply to other portions.
collada	COLLAborative Design Activity; an XML standard for exchange of graphics assets in games and other 3D applications. Originally from	SCEA Shared Source License.

	Sony Computer Entertainment. ".dae" file extension.	
dropbear	SSH server and client.	MIT-like.
expat	An XML parser.	MIT.
freetype	A font engine.	FreeType (BSD-like) or GPL.
giflib	Graphic Interchange Format (GIF) library.	MIT.
harfbuzz	OpenType text shaping engine. Derived from FreeType; developed along with Qt and Pango.	MIT.
icu4c	Internationalization components for Unicode.	ICU (commercial-friendly).
libjpeg	Lossy graphic image file library.	GNU GPL.
libpcap	Packet capture library. Refer also to tcpdump.	New BSD.
libpng	Portable Network Graphics (PNG) image file library.	libpng (commercial-friendly).
libxml2	XML parser library from GNOME.	MIT.
libxslt	XSLT library from GNOME.	MIT.
mesa3d	An Open Source implementation of OpenGL.	Mesa, MIT, and Khronos.
opencv	Open Computer Vision.	BSD.
openssl	Open Secure Sockets Layer.	OpenSSL or SSLeay.
qemu	Processor emulator for x86, PowerPC, ARM, SPARC, and other chips.	GNU GPL.
safe-iop	Safe Integer OPerations library (cross-platform checks for overflow and underflow).	New BSD.
skia	2D graphics library written in C++.	New BSD.
sqlite	SQL database.	Public Domain
tcpdump	TCP packet analyzer. Refer also to libpcap.	New BSD.
tinyxml	A small XML parser.	zlib and libpng (commercial-friendly).
webkit	Web layout engine. Originally developed by Apple. Used in Safari, Chrome, and other browsers.	Mixture of GNU Lesser GPL and BSD.
webrtc	API for realtime audio, video, networking, and signalling.	BSD-like.
zlib	A compression and decompression	zlib (commercial-

	library.	friendly).
wxWidgets	Cross-platform library for building GUI applications. Contains additional classes to deal with many other cross-platform issues such as thread and process management.	wxWindows (commercial-friendly).

Chapter Summary

Many environmental factors can influence the quality of code that comes out of your shop. Developers should not be shy to ask for what they need. It's the manager's job to accommodate these needs as much as possible.

Chapter 6: Development Standards And Specifications

This chapter discusses some of the more common standards that you may need to use or may wish to follow. You will learn some of the details of AUTOSAR, ISO 26262, and MISRA for embedded automotive applications, DO-178, JPL, and JSF for embedded aeronautical applications, and some general purpose coding styling specifications.

General Coding Style

If you are a "cowboy" programmer, you can use any coding style that you please. But, for team development everyone should use the same style mainly to avoid confusion. There are a number of "standard styles" that you can adopt or adapt for your organization including Apache, GNU, Google, and others. Artistic style rules can become a religious war, and nobody will ever win. Be that as it may, pick something that covers these mundane area:

- Indentation including the use of tabs versus spaces. Tabs do not print or display consistently, so I always use spaces.
- Placement of braces ("{" and "}"). Do they go on the same line as the "if" or "while" statement or the next line? How are braces aligned?
- How do you name functions and variables? What are the rules for use of lower and upper case? Underscores?
- What data types can be used?
- How are comments written?
- Where should extra white space always be included? Where should extra white space be avoided?

- What character set should be used in source files? ASCII, UTF-8, UTF-16, other?

In addition to simple style rules, you may be obligated by the nature of your project to use a specific, formal standard in order to comply with industry regulations.

AUTOSAR

AUTomotive Open System ARchitecture[20] (AUTOSAR) is a set of standard platform specifications that have been in development since 2003. The stated goals of the AUTOSAR consortium are:

- Standardization of basic software functionality of automotive Electronic Control Units (ECUs).
- Scalability to different vehicle and platform variants
- Transferability of software.
- Support of different functional domains.
- Definition of an open architecture.
- Collaboration between various partners.
- Development of highly dependable systems.
- Sustainable utilization of natural resources.
- Support of applicable automotive international standards and state-of-the-art technologies.

Although these are platform specifications, you can be sure that when implementing an AUTOSAR device that MISRA and ISO 26262 (both discussed later) will be involved. The goal of AUTOSAR is that all members will provide fully compliant AUTOSAR BSW (Basic SoftWare) modules by 2015.

Practically every kind of sensor, device, and interface that you might find in an ECU is covered: ADC, CAN, DIO, FlexRay, GPT, LIN, MOST, PWM, SPI, XCP, and others. (Even Cryptography— Anti-virus checking software in your car!)

DO-178 / ED-178

These are the standards for the United States / Europe as applied to safety and reliability in airborne avionics systems. They were first introduced in 1992, and the current versions are DO-178C / ED-178C, released in 2011. Related standards are DO-278C / ED-109 for ground-based avionics systems.

These standards emphasize software assurance through a rigorous development process, as opposed to the coding rules. The focus is on:

- Continuous feedback through checklist reviews to ensure that the software meets the low-level requirements.
- Traceability of requirements to code and tests, and traceability between component interactions. The point of this being that no unnecessary code creeps in, and that all requirements have been met.
- The use of qualified development and testing tools.
- Rigorous unit testing. DO-178C allows the use of formal methods as an additional test method.
- The use of a "safe subset" of a high-level programming language. Ada was formerly the defacto standard language, but "C" and C++ are becoming more common.

Software components are divided into five levels of criticality as shown in the following table.

Table 13 - DO-178 Criticality Levels

Level	Failure Type	Description
A	Catastrophic	Error or loss of a critical function required to safely fly or land the aircraft.
B	Hazardous	Failure or large negative impact on safety or performance.
C	Major	Lesser impact than Hazardous, where the incident may result in passenger discomfort as opposed to injury.
D	Minor	Noticeable failure, but with lesser impact. For example, may cause a change in the flight plan, thus inconveniencing passengers.
E	No Effect	Failure has no impact on safety, operating, or crew workload.

The effort required to certify a component is directly related to the criticality level. Higher levels of criticality require more tasks in meeting the quality objectives.

ISO 26262

The ISO 26262[21] standard outlines the entire development process and *Functional Safety* requirements for critical automotive electrical and electronic systems where a failure can result in an accident. ISO 26262 and similar standards for other industries such as medical devices and nuclear power are derived from the broader IEC 61508[22] standard.

The kinds of devices that this standard covers include the Powertrain Control Module, electronic power steering, active suspension, anti-lock brakes, collision prevention, and many others.

The topics covered by ISO 26262 include:

- Automotive safety lifecycle (management, development, production, operation, service, decommissioning), and the necessary activities during these lifecycle phases.

- A risk-based approach for determining risk classes known as Automotive Safety Integrity Levels (ASILs).
- Using ASILs to specify a component's necessary safety requirements for achieving an acceptable residual risk.
- Requirements for validation and confirmation measures to ensure that a sufficient and acceptable level of safety is achieved.

A component's ASIL is a value from A to D, with D being the riskiest. The value is determined from three values:

- Severity. The severity is a four-level class indicating the health effect of a failure. This ranges from no injuries (S1) to life-threatening injuries (S4).
- Probability of Exposure. This is a five-level scale indicating the likelihood that a failure will result in a safety hazard. The scores range from incredible (E0) to highly probable (E4).
- Controllability. This is a four-level scale that measures how well the hazardous condition can be controlled by driver actions or some other external measure. The scores range from generally controllable (C0) to difficult to control or uncontrollable (C4).

The severity, probability, and controllability are then used to look up the ASIL value as in the table below (derived from ISO 26262 Part 3, Table 4). A ranking of "QM" indicates that standard Quality Management is required, but no special action is required in regards to safety.

Table 14 - ISO 26262 ASIL Assignment Matrix

		C1	C2	C3
S1	E1	QM	QM	QM
	E2	QM	QM	QM
	E3	QM	QM	A
	E4	QM	A	B
S2	E1	QM	QM	QM
	E2	QM	QM	A
	E3	QM	A	B
	E4	A	B	C
S3	E1	QM	QM	A
	E2	QM	A	B
	E3	A	B	C
	E4	B	C	D

For ASIL levels A through C, you are obligated to test nothing, every *if* statement, or every *if* branch (both the true and false cases), respectively. For level D you must test 100% of the combinations of operands in an *if* statement, so there a potentially huge number of tests are required. The latter case is referred to as Modified Condition / Decision Coverage (MC/DC) testing.

From the software development standpoint, software development through the use of a Model-based generator tools is encouraged. ISO 26262 also requires extensive unit testing and the collection of reports that can used as evidence in the certification process.

Part 6 of ISO 26262 also has coding guidelines in these areas:

- Minimize code complexity code.
- Use of "safe" language subsets (e.g., MISRA-C).
- Enforce the use of strong types.
- Use defensive programming techniques including parameter validation.

170

- Use established design principles. For example, use "const" not macros in C++, and avoiding the use of global variables that can be confused with local variables.
- Unambiguous graphic representation (does not apply to C/C++).
- Use of style guides.
- Use of naming conventions.

Most Static Analysis tools can be used to detect violations in the items listed above using, for example, a MISRA-C rule checker and other Static Analysis safety checks. Some tools, particularly unit test tools, contain features to create the necessary coverage and traceability reports.

Finally, if you are involved in this industry, your organization will need to become certified. Individuals can become certified as either an Engineer, Professional, or Expert so that you can implement and demonstrate your corporate and product compliance.

JPL

The "JPL Institutional Coding Standard for the C Programming Language"[23] is a superset of MISRA-C:2004 (see below) and other sources. The standard was developed under contract for the National Aeronautics and Space Administration (NASA), and it targets embedded, mission critical flight software.

The JPL standard somewhat modernizes MISRA-C:2004, and it allows you to do some dynamic memory allocation—at least at startup time, use multiple tasks / threads, semaphores, and other features.

JSF

The "Joint Strike Fighter Air Vehicle C++ Coding Standards, December, 2005" is a publicly available document from Lockheed Martin Corporation that is used in the development of software for the F-35 fighter plane.

It is approximately 150 pages long, and defines 220 AV (Air Vehicle) rules, some of which are based on DO-178 and MISRA. A number of the rules are related to style, but a number of the rules also help you to avoid some of the dangerous aspects of C++, especially things that were ambiguous when the original rule lists were designed.

Even if you are not planning to participate in the F-35 fighter program, this is a very useful document for picking up some hints on what is dangerous in C++, and the preferred way of doing something.

LDRA and Polyspace are two Static Analysis products that can check source code against the JSF rule set.

MISRA

The Motor Industry Standard Reliability Association (MISRA) defines several sets of coding rules, which are used in many industries, not just the automotive industry. The available standards are:

- MISRA-C:1998. 127 rules for the C language. Of these, 34 are advisory, and 93 are required for compliance.
- MISRA-C:2004. This extends the 1998 edition with a total of 20 advisory rules, and 122 required for compliance.

- MISRA-C:2012. Extends the above by allowing the use of features from the 1999 "C" standard.
- MISRA-C++:2008. MISRA rules for C++ applications.

MISRA's approach to safety and reliability can be summarized in a few simple concepts:

- Use a restricted, unambiguous set of data types. For example, the size of an "int" (integer) variable depends on the processor and compiler being used. If you are trying to send a message with an "int" from your Airbag Control Unit to the Powertrain Control Module, it probably will not work because one processor is probably 16 bits, and the other is 32 bits. MISRA requires that you say exactly what you mean in the source code, such as uint16 or uint32.
- Avoid the use of dangerous functions and features such as those related to dynamic memory allocation.

At this point in time, the concept of having C++ in a critical automotive application is a bit far-fetched. However, C++ code can be used to write systems that are easier to understand if the code is *well-written*, and you can also implement C++ classes that do not allocate memory left and right.

The "cowboy" in me says "I never want to work on a MISRA-compliant program. I will be bored to death." But, I have also seen some absolutely beautiful, MISRA-C-compliant code for a very complex and critical automotive application.

The full set of MISRA standards costs about US$100.

A number of MISRA rule checking tools are available, and are usually included with high-end development toolkits for embedded applications including those from Green Hills Software, IAR, Renesas Electronics, and others.

Chapter Summary

There are plenty of free coding style guidelines you can use, and a number proprietary specifications that include both recommendations and requirements. Take a look at any that you can get your hands on—they might influence your thinking in regards to style, safety, and quality, and might even give you some new business ideas.

Chapter 7: Design for Portability

"Software Portability" refers to the ease with which you can migrate an application to another operating system or different kind of processor.

If you are never, ever going to try to make your software run on a different architecture, you can skip this chapter. But, think again: maybe in a few years the hardware that you have chosen will become obsolete, or perhaps a new architecture will come out that opens up new markets for you.

Porting to Different Hardware

The main issue when porting to a totally different kind of processor is the size of primitive objects such as integer values and pointers.

The size of an integer usually 16 or 32 bits long, but there is nothing from stopping a compiler writer from deciding that "int" is 64-bits on a 64-bit machine. Therefore, it's important to use C's *typedef* statement to declare exactly what you need (e.g., use a typedef for INT32 instead of just "int"), and isolate those definitions in a platform-specific include file.

It is common to upgrade an application from a smaller processor to a larger processor (e.g., 16 to 32 bits). This is usually a fairly painless exercise. I have had to port the other way (32 to 16), and that's usually very painful. For example, loop counters can easily overflow if proper typedefs have not been used.

Pointers are trickier to deal with because they are not necessarily the same size as integers. On my 64-bit notebook, integers are 32-bits, but pointers are 64-bits. In general, this will not affect nicely written "C", except if you are passing around the pointers to other programs.

I am guilty of this in an application that I never thought I would need to port to a 64-bit architecture. For this application, I absolutely do not need the monstrous memory space available, and most 64-bit systems can run applications designed for "32-bit mode". So a long time ago, even though I knew that using a pointer as an "object handle" in a client-server protocol was not a great idea (for the future)—I did it anyway.

Unfortunately, I recently ran into as situation where I must compile this for a 64-bit environment. Since that would break the client-server protocol, I had to generate a different 32-bit "object handles" and add a lookup table to match an incoming client request with the actual object on the server side. It wasn't that difficult, but wasted some time on something that should have been in the design in the first place.

A final difficulty in porting to new hardware is assembler language. If you must use assembler language, be sure to confine it to a platform-specific module.

Porting to a Different Operating Systems
This can be a lot of work.

Data
For starters, the character sequence used to represent end-of-line can be different. Windows uses carriage return plus line feed, Linux and Unix use line feed, earlier versions of Mac OS use just carriage-return (and, Apple changed it in Mac OS X!). And, here are several other cases. The implication is that

data files, scripts, and possibly source code may need to be converted for use on the other system.

GUI

You may have to do a significant amount of work on any Graphical User Interface. Use of a "portability library" will ease the pain. I first discovered "wxWidgets" when I needed to port some Windows code to run on Linux; the rewrite was very painful. Now I always start creating new applications with a portability library like this, so porting is trivial.

The File System

Another of my favorite booby traps is the #include statement.

One time I was trying to analyze some source code on Linux that was written on Windows and cross-compiled for an embedded application.

There were two problems trying to do the analysis on Linux. First, some of the #include statements used "¥" in path names, whereas the GNU compiler wants to see "/". Those were not so hard to fix. However, the Linux file system is *case-sensitive*, and many of the #included file names were in the wrong case. I gave up—I didn't feel like spending two days editing the code just to run this one tool.

Non-Standard "C"

It is pretty easy to fall into the trap of using compiler-specific functions that do not port. A very common case are the functions strlwr() and strupr() that convert to lower and upper-case respectively. Surprise: these are not standard functions, and they are available only with Microsoft C/C++.

Review the C or C++ standards from time to time to avoid surprises later.

Operating System-Specific Code

If your program is going to do anything at all cool, it will probably have to use some operating system-specific calls.

This is another case where a portability library can help out, so it is worth researching libraries for areas such as process and thread management, tcp/ip communications, web communications, and others.

iOS ←→ Android

Forget it! iOS applications are written in Objective-C, and Android applications are written in Java. You don't port it, you rewrite it.

On iOS you can mix C++ with your Objective-C, and on Android you can use the Native Development Kit (NDK) to call C/C++ from Java, so it may not be a total loss.

Chapter Summary

There are plenty of articles on the Internet and certainly books on the subject of writing portable code. Read them from time to time. Use peer code review with people who have developed for a number of different environments to pick out non-portable code. Finally, always assume that technology *will* change in the future and you may be able to resurrect and adapt a legacy application if it was designed nicely in the first place.

Chapter 8: Analysis Tools

This chapter discusses additional tools you can use besides the compiler and debugger to identify code problems and to improve code quality.

Some screen shots and sample reports are shown for some of the non-proprietary tools.

Dynamic Analysis (DA) Tools

Dynamic Analysis tools execute your program and try to identify bugs in the paths that are exercised. DA tools typically find memory-related problems such as Memory Leaks, Allocation/Deallocation Mismatches, Buffer Overflows, Data Races, and Deadlocks.

Benefits of Dynamic Analysis:

- You can analyze applications with assembler code. (Static Analysis tools generally cannot deal with this.)
- Static Analysis tools cannot analyze concurrency problems well, but Dynamic Analysis tools can do so by detecting thread creation and by monitoring object access.
- A DA tool that provides *code coverage* reports can be used to assist testers and unit test writers, and can be used as evidence in, for example, ISO 26262 certification.

Drawbacks of Dynamic Analysis:

- You must execute something to analyze it, which implies that you must have a complete application. Therefore, Dynamic Analysis is not useful to analyze an incomplete set of code such as a library (although you can certainly use DA with unit test code).
- Dynamic Analysis will only analyze the paths that you specifically exercise.
- Simply executing a specific code path may not necessarily help you find a bug—all of the other conditions for the bug to occur must also be present.
- The application will run slower and will use more memory. This may affect the timing of some operations and therefore disguise some bugs.
- You sometimes need to know what kind of bug you are looking for to enable detection in the tool. If you enable every kind of analysis, the tool is likely to run very slowly.
- If you are not intimately familiar with the source code it is difficult to run tests that will trigger execution through code that you want to test.
- The DA tool may report a problem in your application, but the problem actually occurred in a lower-level library that you have not instrumented for analysis. You may then have to spend a lot of time rebuilding libraries, too, until you can pinpoint the bug.

Free / Open Source DA Tools

clang

The *clang* program is part of the LLVM (Low-level Virtual Machine) project from the University of Illinois at Urbana-

Champaign, and the *clang* portion is a C/C++/Objective-C compiler.

Clang 3.1 and above can generate extra runtime error checks on Linux and Mac OS, but not on Windows. At version 3.1 the option name is "-faddress-sanitizer". From 3.2, the option became "-sanitize=*option_list*", with the main options being "address", "integer", "thread", and "undefined".

Errors that can be detected include NULL Pointer Deference, Use After Free, Array and Buffer bounds, and some inter-thread Race Condition cases. Additionally, some interesting math-related checks can be performed such as integer overflow and shift count checks, although you since this is a DA tool, the error would depend on the input data.

This feature can be used in standalone installations of Clang, with Tizen SDK 2.x, Android NDK version 8 or above, and Xcode 4.3 or above. For other cases, check the version of Clang you are using.

Runtime performance is reasonable. Unfortunately, the current implementation does not contain any Memory Leak checking.

Mudflap
Mudflap is a feature integrated with GNU C/C++ version 4.0 that provides runtime pointer checking for a number of dangerous memory usage cases including memory leaks, NULL pointer dereferences, and buffer overflows.

Mudflap is Open Source and is easy to use, and definitely worth looking at for basic memory error checks. An example of using Mudflap is given in "Memory Leak Detection".

Mtrace

Mtrace is similar to Mudflap, but it is older and it requires that you modify your application to use it.

valgrind

Valgrind is an Open Source application for Linux and Mac OS that runs your application in its own virtual machine. It supports several architectures including x86, PowerPC, and ARM.

It can locate a number of bugs including memory leaks, use after free, buffer overrun, and uninitialized variables.

Drawbacks of valgrind include:

- The application runs 40 to 120 times slower than normal.
- The application will use more than twice as much memory as normal.
- It is known to miss some obvious bugs.
- The messages are fairly cryptic.
- The application actually consists of several sub-tools (memcheck, Helgrind, DRD, and others) which you cannot run at the same time.

The output of valgrind can be overwhelming as it can produce an error report and a stack trace leading up to the error location. Using the "--leak-check=yes" option, I generated more than 15,000 lines of output simply by starting and stopping one application. The error summary at the end of the run is shown below.

```
==2616== LEAK SUMMARY:
==2616==    definitely lost: 9,831 bytes in 54 blocks
==2616==    indirectly lost: 21,098 bytes in 560 blocks
==2616==    possibly lost: 449,964 bytes in 2,278 blocks
==2616==    still reachable: 1,363,785 bytes in 9,041 blocks
==2616==    suppressed: 0 bytes in 0 blocks
==2616== Reachable blocks (those to which a pointer was found) are not
shown.
==2616== To see them, rerun with: --leak-check=full --show-reachable=yes
==2616==
==2616== For counts of detected and suppressed errors, rerun with: -v
==2616== Use --track-origins=yes to see where uninitialised values come
from
==2616== ERROR SUMMARY: 1169 errors from 1081 contexts (suppressed:
3 from 3)
```

You can find more details about this application at
http://www.valgrind.org.

Commercial DA Tools

Intel: Inspector XE 2013

Intel Inspector is a component of the Intel development suite.
Benefits of this tool include:

- Does not require a rebuild to use. It works directly
  with the existing object code, which was preferably
  compiled for a "debug build".
- Works with C, C++, C#, F#, and Fortran.
- Can invoke a debugger when a bug is detected.

Drawbacks of Inspector XE include:

- Code modification may be required when using private memory management or synchronization code.
- Works only with Intel-style CPUs (x86, x86_64).
- Analysis speed is 2 to 320 slower (depending on the analysis type) than running the normal executable.

Parallocity: Zeus Virtual Machine (ZVM)

ZVM version 3.1x is a DA tool that you link to your application and execute in a virtual machine. ZVM is available for both user mode applications and for Linux kernel analysis, and for user mode applications in some BSD-derived versions of Unix.

Benefits of ZVM include:

- ZVM is relatively fast compared to other DA virtual machines.
- Reports generated by the "coverage" option provide a good indication of what has been tested already, so it is easy to determine what else needs to be tested.
- Supports a number of common target processors including x86, x86_64, ARM, MIPS, and PowerPC.
- Can invoke a debugger when a bug is detected.

Drawbacks of ZVM include:

- You must modify the project's "Makefile". This can potentially be awkward for large projects involving nested Makefiles.
- Currently not available for Windows applications.

Static Analysis (SA) Tools

Whereas Dynamic Analysis tools actually execute your program to identify bugs, Static Analysis tools examine the source code.

Benefits of Static Analysis:

- With many tools, it is not necessary to have a complete application in order to run an analysis.
- You do not have to be intimately familiar with the source code in order to find bugs. Static Analysis will automatically identify all paths through the application, as opposed to the paths that you specify during a dynamic test.

Drawbacks of Static Analysis:

- SA will not detect problems introduced by compiler optimization errors. DA might expose these.
- Finding complex bugs depends on the quality of the tool. DA may find leaks that SA tools cannot.

An important distinction between DA and SA is that DA will identify bugs that have actually occurred. For example, DA will identify small memory leaks that do not necessarily crash the application in the paths that you execute, while an SA tool identifies *potential* bugs in the entire application. Therefore, DA is sometimes more useful for focused tests, while SA is better for general quality checks.

How Static Analysis Works

Static Analysis tools can be divided into the following broad categories:

- Rule Checkers. This type of tool checks that the source code is in compliance with a certain set of coding rules such as MISRA-C. While this type of SA tool does not necessarily find bugs, the rules that they are trying to enforce are intended to avoid dangerous programming constructs as well as consistent style.
- Pattern Matchers. This type of tool attempts to find dangerous programming constructs through the use of pattern matching. A simple example of this might be "if (c = getchar())", and the tool will warn that perhaps you wanted "==" in this "if" statement.
- Model Checker. This type of tool expands the source code into a model that can be manipulated more easily than the source code itself, and then attempts to execute the model using symbolic values (instead of real input) to show that the model is valid in all cases. The most popular type of Model Checker is the Boolean Satisfiability Solver ("SAT Solver").
- Theorem Prover. This type of tool attempts to verify program correctness by applying program state assertions at various points in the program. For example, correct pointer usage requires that each pointer has been allocated before it is dereferenced, and that each pointer has been freed prior to termination. Some SA tools provide Automatic Theorem Proving, and hence automatic, internal assertion generation.

Model Checking tools tend to suffer from a "state explosion" problem: the larger the program gets, the more complex the model becomes, and hence the analysis performance degrades. Theorem Proving, in general, tends to be more scalable.

Simple tools detect simple problems. However, they will not detect complex problems such as pointers used incorrectly in linked list and tree structures.

Most advanced tools use a hybrid combination of the techniques mentioned above. For example, for the "if (c == getchar())" example, the tool can simply look at the input to spot a problem—a formal mathematical proof is not required.

Most SA tools work by parsing the source code into a Call Flow Graph. Consider this simple function:

```
const char* MyFunction(int Key)
{
    const char* pszResult;

    if (Key == 0)
        pszResult = "zero";
    else
        pszResult = "non-zero";

    return pszResult;
}
```

This tiny piece of code can be expanded into a Call Flow Graph like this:

Figure 3 - Sample Call Flow Graph

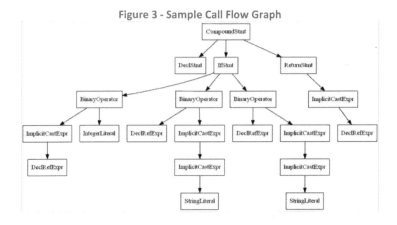

A compiler's job is to examine the declarations and operations so it can then generate machine instructions that are stored in an object file. A Static Analyzer uses the same kind of structure, but instead of generating object code it looks for dangerous situations that compilers usually do not complain about. Some Dynamic Analyzers also use a Call Flow Graph to *instrument* your code. That is, they may add extra safety checks and counters to the generated object code in order to catch bugs at runtime.

False Positives and False Negatives
A *false positive* is a report of a defect that does not actually exist; a *false negative* is the failure to detect a real defect. In statistics these are known as "Type I" and "Type II" errors, respectively.

Tradeoffs need to be made when designing a Static Analysis tool in regards to performance versus precision. Therefore, all Static Analysis tools tend to report some false positives. (The false positive rate varies by product.)

Dynamic Analysis tools theoretically report actual errors and should therefore not report false positives.

False Negatives can occur in either Dynamic or Static Analysis tools—this is simply an indication that the tools is not designed to detect a particular kind of defect, or the tools is not capable of detecting every possible variation of certain kinds of defects.

Free / Open Source SA Tools

clang
Clang (described above) includes built-in components for performing Static Analysis. It can be used as a standalone tool, and is built in to the Xcode IDE for the Mac OS.

Drawbacks of *clang* Static Analysis as of version 3.2 are:

- It can only analyze one function at a time, greatly limiting its value.
- The tool is a work-in-progress.

cppcheck
The cppcheck application can detect a number of bugs including memory leaks, resource leaks, use of dangerous functions, and incorrect use of some Standard Template Library functions.

Benefits of cppcheck include:

- Price (it is free).
- You can customize it without too much difficulty to handle special needs.
- If can identify format string errors in printf(), etc., when running on Windows. (GNU compilers do this for you, but not Microsoft Visual C/C++.)
- Output to GUI application, XML file, or HTML report.

Drawbacks of cppcheck include:

- It mainly uses string pattern matching (regular expressions) and heuristics to perform the analysis, so it cannot identify complex bugs.
- The cppcheck application does not know about "Makefiles" and IDE project files. With basic operation, cppcheck simply scans subdirectories for source code. More complex scanning that limits the analysis to builds based on your macro definitions or builds that use non-default include file settings will require that you understand both your project and cppcheck.

The cppcheck application can be used from the command line or as a GUI application. Below is a screen shot for the GUI application.

Figure 4 - cppcheck-gui Screenshot

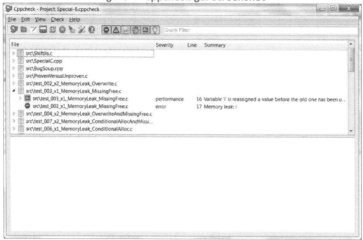

I ran a benchmark of a project with 375,000 lines of "C" and C++ in 1020 files. It was scanned by cppcheck version 1.58 in approximately 15 minutes running with a single thread, and only about 3 minutes using 8 threads.

Commercial SA Tools

There are at least twenty commercial SA tools. Some of the major ones are described below.

Coverity: Prevent

Languages: C, C#, Java.

Coverity is one of the earlier SA tools. My understanding of this product is that it combines a SAT Solver and a Model Checker.

Version 5.2.1 reports approximately 73 different kind of errors, although some of them appear to be redundant to me, some are for obscure, specific cases on specific operating systems, and a number of the reports are disabled by default, presumably because they are not very accurate.

Klocwork: Insight
Languages: C, C++, C#, Java.

My understanding of this product is that it applies Data Flow
Analysis to the Call Flow Graph through a Symbolic Logic
execution engine.

Insight 9.6 has more than 240 error and warning messages.
Quite a few of these are a variation of a single theme, so the
actual number of unique types of errors reported is much
smaller. For example, the messages regarding a "constant
value" in a do, if, switch, or while statement, and "possible
infinite loop" are all basically the same thing.

Mathworks: Polyspace
Languages: C, C++, Ada.

Polyspace uses formal methods and model checking. Its
specialty is detection of math-related errors such as overflow
and division by zero.

Microsoft: Visual C/C++
Languages: C, C++. Refer to Microsoft's FxCop tool for Static
Analysis of C# applications.

The "/analyze" option has been available since CL version
14.00 (Visual Studio 2005), although the feature is not
available in the compiler shipped with all versions of Visual
Studio including the "Professional" and "Express" edition.
(This functionality is available in the compiler shipped with
some versions of the Windows Device Driver Kit, which can be
downloaded separately.)

The analysis tool is based on Microsoft's internally developed
"PREfast" tool, is integrated directly into the compiler, and

provides basic detection of a number of error types discussed in this book.

This tool generates a significant number of false positives, and generates some messages that are very difficult to understand. (The Visual Studio 2012 version claims to improve the false positive rate.) However, it does detect quite a few errors correctly, so it is definitely worth using if you have it.

Monoidics: Infer
Languages: C, C++. Java is planned.

Infer is a newer product that uses formal methods ("Separation Logic") and an automated theorem prover to prove the absence of bugs with respect to the kinds of bugs that it handles. This application focuses mainly on memory-related bugs, but also handles other common errors such as "divide by zero", "resource leaks", and others.

Infer 2.3 reports approximately 30 unique kinds of errors.

Tool Usage Advice
Here are a few tips from my experience in using Static and Dynamic Analysis tools.

Use Your Tools Regularly
You need to use your tools regularly to become familiar with how they behave so that you can easily sift through any generated noise. No analysis tool is perfect, so it is not uncommon to use multiple tools.

Debug versus Release Build
Consider the following code that uses the assert() macro:

```
void MyFunc(char* p)
{
    assert(p != NULL);
    *p = '¥0';
}
```

This code will likely generate an analysis error in the Release build because the assert macro only generates a safety check for "p" in the Debug build. You can therefore avoid annoying error messages such as "p might be NULL" (which would *not* be a false positive in the Release build) by verifying against the Debug build. However, it is your problem to determine if you can really omit the safety check in the Release version!

Analyze Modules and Then Packages

It is totally plausible that the module you are in charge of is *perfect*—that is until the person sitting in the next cubicle who is working on code that consumes your module uses it in some totally bizarre way that you never intended.

An example of where this can happen is with Memory Leaks. When some library code allocates some memory, who is responsible for freeing it? The analysis tool is not a mind reader, and cannot decipher usage comments in the code, either. Therefore, analysis of the library might show that the module is safe. However, the person using the module may not have read the instructions (or the instructions may not even exist yet), so when you plug the modules together an error may occur.

You can avoid these problems by having everyone analyze their own code at the desktop, and then analyze the overall project during daily master builds.

Will Analysis Tools Help Here?

Analysis tools will not help in every situation. Some examples are described below.

In 2013, Chrysler Corporation made several recalls related to software. One was for airbag and seatbelt problems in some models of Jeeps, transmission problems in other models of Jeeps, and deployment of the wrong airbag in some models of Dodge Ram cargo vans. In the latter case, the software was testing the sensor on the wrong side of the car. There is completely no way for an analysis tool to detect this. Only really good eyes during a code review or live testing will expose this.

Also in 2013, Honda recalled 44,000 Fit Sport cars due to a flaw in the software for the Vehicle Stability Assist. Apparently, the control data was created using the parameters for one particular brand of tire, but the VSA did not respond appropriately when another brand of tires were used. No tool is going to detect this. Does this also imply that every time you buy new tires that you need to get your car reprogrammed?

In 2007, during the first deployment of F-22 Raptors overseas, the navigation and communications systems on six planes flying from Hawaii to Japan went berserk when they crossed the International Date Line. The planes managed to return safely, and the problem was repaired within 48 hours. There are probably no tools that would have found this, but didn't the developers ever think about testing this code?

The Industrial Control Systems Cyber Emergency Response Team recently released an alert (ICS-ALERT-0130-164-01) that warns about hard-coded passwords in various medical devices. Since many people know the password, it would be easy for someone to hack the machine and do various nefarious things such as changing the dosage on a drug injection machine. Catching this in any single analysis tool would be very difficult, and this alert involved over 300 machines, 40 manufacturers, and probably quite a few different operating systems.

Chapter Summary

Static Analysis tools can take a long time to run, but you can run it up front and then take your time to review the results. If you use an SA tool during development, fixing problems is usually trivial. If you analyze an existing application, you are likely to find obscure bugs that are difficult to trigger. Developers with time constraints, but not risk constraints, sometimes ignore less critical bugs.

Dynamic Analysis tools can be run more like a debugger once you have the application running a little bit. However, DA tools run much slower than the normal executable, and the speed difference can be very annoying. You are likely to find bugs that you were not even expecting such a buffer overrun once you exercise the right blocks of code.

Use of both Static Analysis and Dynamic Analysis tools will definitely help you find difficult to spot bugs, so using any tools that you can is highly recommended.

Chapter 9: In Hindsight...

Here are some of my more interesting debugging experiences. Advanced analysis tools or a different approach might have helped to solve the problem faster—but not always.

Crash At End of Call

Some code that I do not recall having changed for a few years started getting Access Violations at the end of a telephone call. I was at least able to get a stack trace by catching the Access Violations, but the location was inconsistent. It was difficult to reproduce, and it was occurring on a system without any development tools installed. A few times, when I thought I had narrowed in on the problem, I added some debugging messages. However, that seemed to change the timing, and then I could not generate the error.

Putting the program back to normal without the extra debug messages, the error started happening again. But, this time I also updated the associated ".PDB" (program database), and got a nice stack trace including line numbers of all of the calls.

The stack trace showed that there was a sprint() type of problem, which usually means there is a format mismatch. Aha, the format string for the Japanese version must be wrong! But, it was okay.

That left the possibility that the format string was NULL. How could that be?

I went up a few levels, and found a routine that was being called several times, but in one case, one of the parameters was different. Why?

It was different because the code *had* been changed *a few years ago*, this particular parameter had not been updated properly in the new code, and the bug just happened to show up a few years later in the extreme case that I had triggered.

The problem was that I did not do enough corner-case testing. It would have taken some very perverse unit tests to expose this particular bug. Obviously, I needed to do more testing in the first place, but how much is enough for a relatively low-volume product?

Lost Payroll

The batch processing subsystem at my university was replaced with a new product that promised to be more efficient. It did this, but with one catch: jobs were sometimes submitted with no indication of an error, and they would immediately vanish into the ether.

Student's lab assignments would sometimes get lost, and we could only say "Sorry, please resubmit it." When it came to more serious jobs such as grade reports and payroll, though, a "tough luck" response was not acceptable.

There were a number of places where the failure could be occurring.

- PDP-8. Remote site controller for terminals, card reader, and printer. Is the job really being sent?
- PDP-11. Handles traffic between the remote sites and the mainframe. What is actually going on here? Receiving the job? Forwarding to the mainframe?
- PDP-10. Is this receiving the job? Is the job in the queue?

This was a horrible to figure out. For starters, the PDP-8s were in remote locations, but fortunately two were within walking distance on campus. These machines had almost no debugging facilities, except you could set hardware breakpoints and examine some data with the toggle switches and lights. And, all of the code was written in an assembler language that I was not familiar with when I started looking at the problem.

I fortunately solved the problem before I had to look into the PDP-11, but this was also another set of assembler code that I was only vaguely familiar with.

Finally, there was the PDP-10 that actually ran the batch system, which in turn ran user jobs. All system-level code was written in yet another assembler language, although this one I was intimately familiar with.

So the situation was:

- User submits a deck of cards through the card reader spooler.
- The job is transmitted from PDP-8, to PDP-11, to PDP-10, where it is submitted to the job queue.
- The batch master process selects next job to run— except—it's gone!

Problem 1: *Nobody* was familiar with the innards of the new batch system—it had just been released, and I think we were one of the first installations.

Problem 2: We had limited system-level debugging time. This had to occur between 5am and 6am, and no more than twice a week.

Problem 3: The batch control programs were background processes that were difficult to debug.

Problem 4: The problem happened randomly, even with the same input.

So, where to start? This was a long time ago, but I am sure I spent a little time looking at the batch system in the PDP-10. Then, at some point, I wanted to know if the job was being *sent*, so I started looking at the far end (the PDP-8). That ate up quite a bit of time, and that was another system that I couldn't just hack at will because that would have interfered with all of the users at the remote site.

At some point I went back to the PDP-10, and figured out how to peek at incoming jobs in the debugger. This was rather intense debugging because you had to peek at things for a few seconds, and then let the system continue to avoid timeouts in other places.

While looking at this data, I stumbled upon a mysterious set of per-job flag bits, one of which meant "delete this job". And, sometimes, this bit was already set, so the control program would silently delete the incoming job!

I finally tracked the "delete me" bit back to the card reader spooler. This program was expanding memory once in a while. When a new job came through, the card reader spooler would reuse the previously expanded memory *without reinitializing it*, and once in a while the uninitialized memory just happened to end up in the "delete me" flag.

This took a very long time to figure out, and the fix was ridiculously simple: zero the work memory in the card reader spooler before each job.

I was somewhat of a hero for figuring this out, but what could I have done to speed up the debugging? Perhaps:

- I spent too much time looking at a low level. I learned a lot of unrelated things about the PDP-8, but that was a waste of time in solving the problem. The card reader spooler actually ran on the mainframe (which I didn't understand when I started). I should have first concentrated on what I knew, and tried to show that the job was or was not received correctly.
- I probably should have made some diagrams, and probably should have tried to explain the problem to somebody else.
- I should have added some basic, high-level log messages to the batch system right from the beginning. For various reasons (assembler language, limited access time, etc.), I did not do this.

Delete *.*

Somebody discovered once that wildcard file name handling was handled only by the command line processor, and not by the operating system.

That meant that with a few lines of assembler code you could actually create files with strange names like "*.doc".

Some wise guy decided one day to create a file named "*.*" in his buddy's directory. When his buddy tried to logout, he was over is disk quota, as usual, and the logout program started prompting him for files to delete:

Do you want to delete *.bak? Y
Do you want to delete *.obj? Y
Do you want to delete *.*? *Please STOP!!!!*

Lessons learned: Code defensively. Normal people will always do absolutely stupid things to your system either out of ignorance or by accident. Evil people *try* to do stupid things to see how clever the system is. [John, I am sorry that I almost gave you a heart attack, and I am so glad that you didn't fall for this stupid prank.]

Canibal.exe

One of my customer's disgruntled employees modified their system, and restarted it. Part of the modification included a not-so-nice feature that deleted both the source and object code.

The next time the system had to be restarted, the employee was long gone, and naturally there was no backup.

Lessons learned: Besides being nicer to your employees so they don't do bad things like this in the first place, you should personally verify that you actually have backups!

(The person who did this subsequently dared to call me up looking for a job. I think my response was something like "Please leave the country because if I get my hands on you...")

The Customer is Always Right

A customer couldn't get our software installed, and insisted that she was an experienced user. After hours on the phone, we were finally able to exactly match up the hardware configuration in question. It turns out that the customer was stupid mistaken, and ~~didn't know the difference between~~ was confusing colon (":") and semicolon (";").

Lessons learned: (1) Patience is a virtue, and we are still patiently waiting for this person to say "thank you", and (2) Even though you want to save ink and trees, making all of those silly little screenshots in the documentation can be sometimes pay off. This incident happened during the days of MS-DOS and dot-matrix printers, but it is easy to do now.

Two Hundred Angry New Users

We provided the server part of a big telephone system once, and practically all of the users were immediately very unhappy about something. It bubbled up to top management that our software was horrible.

It turned out that the company who made the client part of the system put *our* software name on *their* screen, and *their* software had some glitches in it. The users didn't know the difference, so they blamed what they saw on the screen.

Lessons learned? We were friendly with the other company, but I hadn't really gotten around to checking out their application. Be careful about how other people use your trademarks, friendly partner or not.

How Many Unit Tests Is Enough?

We made a very cool fax system once, and the customer was very happy with it, except once in a blue moon, a fax that was received correctly would not be forwarded, supposedly because the file was broken.

It took us a while to capture one of these cases, and then I had to figure out in what respect it was broken. The captured file was definitely not broken.

After many, many hours of experimentation, I found the problem. You are not going to believe this: If the file size was a multiple of 192, 193, or 194 bytes, a bug in the LAN driver caused the final block to be copied incorrectly when we moved the file from the fax system to the file server. (This was in age of Novell LANs when you could spend half of your life finding driver updates on CompuServe.)

There is a big lesson here, and it is not a happy one. This was not our bug, but it showed up in our system so we had to worry about it. In any case, how can a developer test this? Test sending a file of every size from 0 to 4GB? It also requires having *exactly* (repeat *exactly*) the same system configuration including computers, software, software versions (including drivers), and LAN cards. This will not happen for most one-off systems.

The lesson: I don't know. Deal only with reasonable customers who won't go insane with a system problem that you don't know what it is.

Take Two Aspirin, Please
Patient: "Doctor, I don't feel well."

Doctor: "Tell me where it hurts."

Patient: "You're the doctor, you tell me!"

Actually, I have customers who are concerned with customer data security. No problem, I can appreciate that.

What drives me crazy, though, is when they want to know what happened to a particular telephone call, and usually they want to know "Did the customer hang up on purpose or by accident, or was the customer service agent rude?" This question comes up about once a year. To trace the call, I need the log file, which is very large. Then, I need to follow the call all over the place because it may have been transferred several times, and there are potentially hundreds of messages to look at because all customers insist on turning on the highest level of log details even though it says in the manual and on the configuration screen that for performance reasons this is not recommended.

Depending on the mood of the person we request the log from, sometimes the reply is "No, you cannot have the log file because it contains private customer information." (The log file has telephone numbers in it, but no names or other private data.)

We have non-disclosure agreements with our customers, and have no desire to call the numbers in the log file. So, we are the doctor, the patient doesn't have any obvious injuries, and we're suppose to guess what happened? Good grief! Usually we end up with the log, but the exercise is such a waste of time.

Oh no—I just had a ridiculous idea how to deal with customers like this. How about encrypting the telephone numbers and similar information. We will get something that we can search for in the logs, and the customer can decrypt it if they really need to see the data. Wow! Can I patent this? Never mind.

By the way, the reason the call gets disconnected is invariably that the customer hung up because the cat jumped on the phone, a mobile phone went out of range, or a mobile phone's battery ran out. We have yet to detect a case where the agent hung up first.

Free Big Willy
This one is for your amusement.

We sold a lot of systems one year that ended up being used in an adult-themed business. This wasn't the intended use of the system, but the money involved was very enticing.

There was a problem with one of the systems where it would mysteriously start clicking the speaker and then become unresponsive for about 30 seconds. Then it would just continue normally.

I suspected that a device driver was sometimes leaving interrupts disabled, but I was never able to prove this. In the meantime, I had to listen, for an entire week, to this adult content that was describing some guy's private body parts. This quickly became boring, and it was extremely embarrassing when somebody came by my workspace on the way to the kitchen.

The technical issues here are: (1) How do you catch the system state without changing the system?, and (2) How do you trigger "random behavior"?

I don't think I ever resolved this. This is sometimes hard to do, but it is useful to put some kind of health indicators in the user interface. This won't fix the problem, but will perhaps help to determine which part of the program has gone haywire.

Chapter Summary
This chapter was mostly for fun. I am sure you have plenty interesting tales, yourself.

Chapter 10: Debugging Tips

This chapter contains some compiler and debugger-specific tips and tricks you can use to track down some kinds of bugs.

GNU C/C++

Extra Software Tools for Linux

Most Linux distributions including CentOS, Fedora, Red Hat, and SuSE tend to come with lots of development tools preinstalled. I happen to use Ubuntu frequently, a distribution that is more oriented toward general use. Below is most of the script that I use to set up an Ubuntu system.

```
#! /bin/bash
sudo apt-get install -y build-essential
sudo apt-get install -y bison
sudo apt-get install -y bjam  # Used by boost
sudo apt-get install -y autoconf
sudo apt-get install -y autogen
sudo apt-get install -y automake
sudo apt-get install -y curl
sudo apt-get install -y dos2unix  # Fixes newline problems
sudo apt-get install -y flex
# sudo apt-get install -y ftjam
sudo apt-get install -y gawk
sudo apt-get install -y gcc-multilib g++-multilib # 32-bit headers
sudo apt-get install -y git-core  # Another source code control system
sudo apt-get install -y gperf
sudo apt-get install -y gruff # Used in some documentation builds
# sudo apt-get install -y jam  #Another build system
sudo apt-get install -y libtool
sudo apt-get install -y libxml2-dev # Contains xmllint
sudo apt-get install -y mercurial # Source code control for Mozilla
sudo apt-get install -y mono-complete  #.Net runtime
sudo apt-get install -y libncurses5-dev lib32ncurses5-dev
```

208

```
sudo apt-get install -y python  # Probably installed via build-essential
sudo apt-get install -y texinfoc
sudo apt-get install -y xsltproc  # Used in Android builds
sudo apt-get install -y yasm
sudo apt-get install -y libz-dev lib32z-dev

if [[ $BITS =~ "86_64" ]]; then
    sudo apt-get install -y ia32-libs
else
    echo "(No 32-bit-only packages to install)"
fi
```

If you are not up to speed on using Linux, you should master the following commands right away:

- Compilers: gcc, g++, and perhaps clang and clang++.
- Linker: ld.
- Debugger: gdb.
- Archive handler: tar. Use "tar xf filename.tar" to expand a .tar file, and "tar xzf filename.tar.gz" to expand a gzipped tar file. There are many other options.
- Search for files: find. Usually "find . –name *"filename_pattern"*. There are many other advanced handling options.
- Search for text: grep. My favorite tool on the planet.
- List symbols in object file: nm.

Get yourself a good editor, or use Eclipse or another decent IDE. Using vi, vim, and gedit are very painful for software development work.

GNU Debugger Quick Reference
- gdb *executable* —debug a program.

209

- b *filename:line* or *procedure:z* – set a breakpoint.
- bt – display stack backtrace.
- c – continue execution from breakpoint.
- clear – delete breakpoint at next instruction.
- delete [*n*] – delete all breakpoints, or delete breakpoint "*n*".
- n – execute next line, skipping function calls.
- p [*/format*] variable – print a variable. The *format* can be c, d, u, x and other options for character, decimal, unsigned, hexadecimal, etc.
- quit – exit the debugger.
- run – start execution.
- s – execute next line, entering any called functions.

Memory Leak Detection

To find memory leaks you will need to use a separate tool such as mtrace, mudflap, valgrind, or some of the other Static or Dynamic Analysis tools discussed in this book.

Minimally, you can use Mudflap. This is available since GNU C/C++ version 4.0 that provides runtime pointer checking for a number of dangerous memory usage cases.

Mudflap is dependent on the compiler version. On Ubuntu, for example, you can install Mudflap for GNU 4.6 with:

sudo apt-get install libmudflap0-4.6-dev

Next, you compile your code with the -fmudflap option to cause extra pointer checking code to be generated, and you link with the "mudflap" library ("mudflapth" for multi-threaded applications). Then, you set the desired Mudflap runtime options and run your program. For example:

```
gcc -g -fmudflap myApp.c -lmudflap -o myApp
export MUDFLAP_OPTIONS=-print-leaks
./myApp
```

Memory leaks are reported with output such as this:

```
*******
mudflap violation 1 (unregister): time=1358636595.668159 ptr=0x16c2420
size=0
pc=0x7f3ef2477e36
number of nearby objects: 0
Leaked object 1:
mudflap object 0x16c1e50: name=`malloc region'
bounds=[0x16c1d90,0x16c1df3] size=100 area=heap check=0r/0w liveness=0
alloc time=1358636595.668025 pc=0x7f3ef2478291
    /usr/lib/x86_64-linux-gnu/libmudflap.so.0(__mf_register+0x41)
[0x7f3ef2478291]
    /usr/lib/x86_64-linux-gnu/libmudflap.so.0(__wrap_malloc+0xe2)
[0x7f3ef2478fe2]
    ./test(main+0x19) [0x4007bd]  (Memory was allocated here.)
    /lib/x86_64-linux-gnu/libc.so.6(__libc_start_main+0xed) [0x7f3ef20d176d]
number of leaked objects: 1
```

While the output is not gorgeous, just the ability to get the report with a free tool is a certainly great help in debugging. You can find detailed information about Mudflap in the GNU documentation.

MALLOC_CHECK_

According to the Linux documentation for malloc(), you can set the environment variable "MALLOC_CHECK_" to enable some very basic malloc-related error checks when using libc version 5.4.23 or higher, and glibc 2.x or higher.

I was unable to make this do anything at all on my system.

Exception Handling

The following sample code catches floating point and segment violation exceptions.

```
#define _GNU_SOURCE
#include <execinfo.h>
#include <stdio.h>
#include <stdlib.h>
#include <string.h>
#include <unistd.h>
#include <signal.h>
#include <setjmp.h>
#include <fenv.h>

/*
    Boo:  Return behavior is undefined for the signals we're most interested in.
    Boo:  Static functions don't appear in the trace.
    Boo:  Doesn't show recursion.  (It could at least show "...repeated <n> times".)
    Boo:  No line numbers.
    Boo:  You can introduce timing-related security problems with signal+longjmp.
        (https://www.securecoding.cert.org/confluence/display/seccode/SIG32-
C.+Do+not+call+longjmp()+from+inside+a+signal+handler)
*/

/* You need need to handle exceptions on a per-thread basis, and will need
    different buffers for each thread.  You may also need a list (stack) of
    buffers to handle things nicely.

    Also, "The distinction between setjmp() or longjmp() and sigsetjmp() or siglongjmp()
    is only significant for programs which use sigaction(), sigprocmask() or sigsuspend()."

*/

sigjmp_buf MainJumpBuff;

void Backtrace(void)
{
    int j;
    int nptrs;
    void *buffer[20];
    //char **strings;

    nptrs = backtrace(buffer, sizeof buffer / sizeof buffer[0]);

    // Print directly to stderr.  You get also call backtrace_symbols() to get
    // an array of strings (which you must then free).  However, that would
    // call malloc(), which might indirectly have been related to the original
```

```
   // problem that we're trying to trace!

   backtrace_symbols_fd(buffer, nptrs, 2);
}

void myfunc(int WhichError, int ncalls)
{
   if (ncalls > 1) {
      // Call myself recursively a few times to build up the stack
      myfunc(WhichError, ncalls - 1);
   }
   else {
      if (WhichError == 1) {
         float f1 = 1.0f;
         float f2 = 0.0f;
         f1 = f1 / f2;
         printf("Result = %f\n", f1);
      }
      else {
         char* p = NULL;
         memcpy(p, "You are dead", 13);
      }
   }
}

void SignalHandler(int Signal /*, int subcode: gcc specific parameter*/)
{
   switch(Signal) {
      case SIGFPE:
         printf("Signal SIGFPE received\n");
         Backtrace();
         siglongjmp(MainJumpBuff, 1);
         //break;
      case SIGSEGV:
         printf("Signal SIGSEGV received\n");
         Backtrace();
         siglongjmp(MainJumpBuff, 2);
         //break;
      default:
         printf("Signal %d received\n", Signal);
         break;
   }
}

int main(int argc, char *argv[])
{
   int itemp;
   int setjmpResult;
   char szLine[80];
   int WhichError;
```

```
/* NOTES:
   fenableexcept is gcc-specific.

   sigaction() should be used in new applications instead of signal().
*/

(void)feclearexcept(FE_ALL_EXCEPT); /* (should really be clear already!) */
(void)feenableexcept(FE_INVALID|FE_DIVBYZERO|FE_OVERFLOW|FE_UNDERFLOW);
(void)signal(SIGFPE, SignalHandler);

(void)signal(SIGSEGV, SignalHandler);

while(printf("1=SIGFPE, 2=SIGSEGV, ^D to exit: "), fgets(szLine, sizeof szLine, stdin) != NULL) {
    WhichError = atoi(szLine);
    if (WhichError >= 1 && WhichError <= 2) {
        setjmpResult = sigsetjmp(MainJumpBuff, 1);
        switch(setjmpResult) {
            case 0:
                myfunc(WhichError, 5);
                break;
            case 1:
                printf("Ouch: SIGFPE!\n");
                /* Reenable */
                (void)feclearexcept(FE_ALL_EXCEPT);
                (void)feenableexcept(FE_INVALID|FE_DIVBYZERO|FE_OVERFLOW|FE_UNDERFLOW);
                (void)signal(SIGFPE, SignalHandler);
                break;
            case 2:
                printf("Ouch: SIGSEGV!\n");
                /* Reenable -- hmmm: Somebody disables floating point exceptions when we
                   get a segment fault! */
                (void)feclearexcept(FE_ALL_EXCEPT);
                (void)feenableexcept(FE_INVALID|FE_DIVBYZERO|FE_OVERFLOW|FE_UNDERFLOW);
                (void)signal(SIGSEGV, SignalHandler);
                break;
            default:
                printf("setjmp returned unabled value %d\n", setjmpResult);
                break;
        }
    }
}

putchar('\n');
return 0;
}
```

Microsoft C/C++

Extra Software Tools for Windows

Here are some extra software tools you can use to assist in you development and debugging:

- Disassembler: dumpbin.exe. In additional to disssembling code, you can list import and export symbols. Included with Visual Studio.
- Unix/Linux tools. Get a copy of MinGW, Cygwin, or both. MinGW allows you to build native Windows applications using the GNU tool chain and command line utilities. Cygwin is similar, and provides a Posix emulation layer to allow you to port Unix/Linux applications to run on Windows. I prefer MinGW because Cygwin has a GNU license, so there are so redistribution restrictions for commercial applications.

Debugging

Memory dumps, thread control, and many other debug-related actions are available from the Debug menu in Visual Studio.

Breakpoints can also be set from the Debug menu, or by moving the cursor to the desired line and pressing the F9 key.

Memory Leak Detection

The debug runtime supports memory leak detection and reporting by adding code such as this in the startup code of your application:

```
#include <crtdbg.h>
#if defined(_DEBUG) && defined(WIN32)
_CrtSetDbgFlag (_CRTDBG_ALLOC_MEM_DF |
_CRTDBG_LEAK_CHECK_DF);
_CrtSetReportMode(_CRT_ERROR,_CRTDBG_MODE_DEBUG);
#endif
```

When you next debug the application, you may see messages such as this when you exit:

```
Detected memory leaks!
Dumping objects ->
{115} normal block at 0x002D0068, 100000 bytes long.
Data: <    > CD CD CD CD CD CD CD CD CD CD CD CD CD CD CD CD
Object dump complete.
```

In this case the memory allocated on the 115th call to malloc() was not freed. The next step is to add this line in your startup code:

```
_CrtSetBreakAlloc(115);
```

You now debug the application *again*, and when malloc() is called the 115th time, the debugger will stop with a breakpoint in malloc(). From here, you can usually trace back to source that allocated the object, and then you can decide how and where to fix it.

216

You may luck out if you can recognize the contents of the data. Is it a meaningful string or integer value? Or, perhaps the size of the leaked block gives you a hint as to what it is?

When the allocation number is not constant, perhaps because the allocation is timing-dependent, this technique gets a lot trickier.

Exception Handling

Here are a few routines I use for catching Structured Exceptions such as Access Violations in a Windows Application.

```
#include "stdafx.h"
#include "Teleplex.h"
#include "Exception.h"
#include <TPXAppLog.h>

#ifdef _DEBUG
#define DEBUG_NEW new(_NORMAL_BLOCK, __FILE__, __LINE__)
#define new DEBUG_NEW
#undef THIS_FILE
static char THIS_FILE[] = __FILE__;
#endif

int          gExceptionCount = 0;    // Exceptions detected (hopefully ZERO)

static void    ExceptionStackTrace(CONTEXT* pContext);

int TPXAPI ExceptionHandler(void* pException)
///////////////////////////////////////////////////////////////////////
// NAME:         Exceptionhandler
//
// DESCRIPTION:  General exception handler.  Should be used only
//                 for the runtime portion of Teleplex.
///////////////////////////////////////////////////////////////////////
{
   ULONG       dwAddress;
   ULONG       dwTID;
```

```
extern int     gExceptionCount;
extern CTPXCfg  *gpTPXCfg;
CONTEXT        *pContext;
TCHAR          *pszAccessMode;
LPCTSTR         pszThreadName;
struct _EXCEPTION_RECORD *pXR;
int      rc = EXCEPTION_CONTINUE_SEARCH;
TCHAR          szMsg[1024];
EXCEPTION_POINTERS* xp = (EXCEPTION_POINTERS*)pException;


pXR = xp->ExceptionRecord;


gExceptionCount++;        // Count these just in case we're in a bad loop
dwTID = ::GetCurrentThreadId();


pContext = xp->ContextRecord;

if (pXR->ExceptionCode != EXCEPTION_ACCESS_VIOLATION) {
    pszAccessMode = _T("");
    dwAddress = 0;
}
else {
    pszAccessMode = pXR->ExceptionInformation[0] == 0 ? "Read" : "Write";
    dwAddress = pXR->ExceptionInformation[1];
}

if (ThreadInfo.m_pszName == NULL)
    pszThreadName = _T("unknown");
else
    pszThreadName = ThreadInfo.m_pszName;


_stprintf(szMsg,_T("XCPT=%#x,Thread=%s,TID=%#x,ExceptAddr=%#x,Mode=%s,Addr
=%#x"),
        pXR->ExceptionCode,
        pszThreadName,
        dwTID,
        pXR->ExceptionAddress,
        pszAccessMode,
        dwAddress);
    gAppLog.LogMsg(LOGF_ALWAYS,szMsg);

    TPXAlert(0,ALERT_CAT_XCPT,szMsg,NULL,NULL);

#if defined(_M_IX86)
```

```
        gApplog.LogMsg(LOGF_ALWAYS,
            "GS=%#x,FS=%#x,ES=%#x,DS=%#x",
            pContext->SegGs,
            pContext->SegFs,
            pContext->SegEs,
            pContext->SegDs);
        gApplog.LogMsg(LOGF_ALWAYS,
            "EDI=%#x,ESI=%#x,EAX=%#x,EBX=%#x,ECX=%#x,EDX=%#x",
            pContext->Edi,
            pContext->Esi,
            pContext->Eax,
            pContext->Ebx,
            pContext->Ecx,
            pContext->Edx);
        gApplog.LogMsg(LOGF_ALWAYS,
            "EBP=%#x,CS:EIP=%#x:%#x,FLAGS=%#x,SS:ESP=%#x:%#x",
            pContext->Ebp,
            pContext->SegCs,
            pContext->Eip,
            pContext->EFlags,
            pContext->SegSs,
            pContext->Esp);
#endif  // x386

        ExceptionStackTrace(pContext);    // make a stack trace

        rc = EXCEPTION_EXECUTE_HANDLER;
        return rc;
}
static void ExceptionStackTrace(CONTEXT *pContext)
/////////////////////////////////////////////////////////////////////
// NAME:        ExceptionStackTrace
//
// DESCRIPTION:    Perform a stack trace for the current exception.
//          If this is a repeated exception (same thread
//          and exception address), the trace is skipped
//          because the trace is somewhat time-consuming.
/////////////////////////////////////////////////////////////////////
{
        static ULONG   dwLastEIP;
        static ULONG   dwLastThreadID;
        ULONG          dwThreadID;

        gApplog.m_IOCriticalSection.Lock();
```

```
dwThreadID = ::GetCurrentThreadId();
if (dwThreadID != dwLastThreadID && pContext->Eip != dwLastEIP) {
    dwLastThreadID = dwThreadID;
    dwLastEIP = pContext->Eip;

    DumpStack(GetCurrentThread(),pContext);
}

gAppLog.m_lOCriticalSection.Unlock();
}
```

Chapter Summary

This chapter has presented a few tips and tricks for common development environments.

References

[1] "Elements of Programming Style", B. W. Kernighan and P. J. Plauger, McGraw-Hill, New York, 1974. ISBN-0-07-034199-0.

[2] "Secure Coding in C and C++", Robert C. Seacord, Addison-Wesley, 2005.

[3] Libmpdec (Decimal Arithmetic Library), http://www.bytereef.org/mpdecimal.

[4] "ANSI/IEEE Std 754, IEEE Standard for Binary Floating-Point Arithmetic", 1985.

[5] "ISO/IEC 9899:TC2, Programming Languages – C", May 2005 (Committee Draft).

[6] Waterfall Model, http://en.wikipedia.org/wiki/Waterfall_model.

[7] "Crystal Clear, A Human-Powered Methodology for Small Teams", Alistair Cockburn, October 2004, Addison-Wesley Professional, ISBN 978-0201699470.

[8] Dynamic Systems Development Method (DSDM) Consortium, http://www.dsdm.org.

[9] DSDM online store, http://www.dsdm.org/dig-deeper.

[10] Extreme Programming, http://en.wikipedia.org/wiki/Extreme_Programming.

[11] "Extreme Programming Refactored: The Case Against XP", Matt Stephens and Doug Rosenberg, August 2003, Springer-Verlag, ISBN 978-1-59059-096-6.

[12] "Java Modeling In Color With UML: Enterprise Components and Process", Peter Coad, Jeff de Luca, and Eric Lefebvre, June 1999, Prentice Hall International, ISBN 978-0-13011-510-2.

[13] "Lean Software Development: An Agile Toolkit, Mary Poppendieck and Tom Pollendieck", May 2003, Addison-Wesley Professional, ISBN 978-0321150783.

[14] Rapid Application Development (RAD). http://en.wikipedia.org/wiki/Rapid_application_development.

[15] Scrum Alliance. http://www.scrumalliance.org.

[16] Scrum (development).

http://en.wikipedia.org/wiki/Scrum_(development).
[17] "Toyota Production System, An Integrated Approach to Just-In-Time", Yasuhiro Monden, 2011 (4th edition), Productivity Press, ISBN 978-1439820971.
[18] List of Software Development Philosophies. http://en.wikipedia.org/wiki/List_of_software_development_philosophies.
[19] Comparison of Documentation Generators, http://en.wikipedia.org/wiki/Comparison_of_documentation_generators.
[20] AUTOSAR, Bernhard-Wicki-Strasse 3, 80636 Munich, Germany. http://www.autosar.org.
[21] "ISO 26262-*xx*: 2011 -- Road vehicles – Functional safety – Part *xx*", International Organization for Standardization, Geneva, Switzerland, November, 2011. There are 10 different parts.
[22] "IEC 61508-x ed2.0 (2010-04) Functional Safety of Electrical /Electronic / Programmable Electronic Safety-related Systems – Part *x*," International Electrotechnical Commission, Geneva, Switzerland, April, 2010. There are 7 different parts.
[23] "JPL Institutional Coding Standard for the C Programming Language", Jet Propulsion Laboratory, University of California, Pasdenda, California, March, 2009.

Printed in Great Britain
by Amazon